YOUR PERSONAL ASTROLOGY PLANNER

PISCES 2008

YOUR PERSONAL ASTROLOGY PLANNER

PISCES 2008

RICK LEVINE & **JEFF** JAWER

STERLING
New York / London
www.sterlingpublishing.com

Library of Congress Cataloging-in-Publication Data Available

2 4 6 8 10 9 7 5 3 1

Published by Sterling Publishing Co., Inc.
387 Park Avenue South, New York, NY 10016

Distributed in Canada by Sterling Publishing
c/o Canadian Manda Group, 165 Dufferin Street
Toronto, Ontario, Canada M6K 3H6
Distributed in the United Kingdom by GMC Distribution Services
Castle Place, 166 High Street, Lewes, East Sussex, England BN7 1XU
Distributed in Australia by Capricorn Link (Australia) Pty. Ltd.
P.O. Box 704, Windsor, NSW 2756, Australia

Original book design: 3+Co., New York

Manufactured in the United States of America

Sterling ISBN-13: 978-1-4027-4849-3
ISBN-10: 1-4027-4849-3

TABLE OF CONTENTS

THE PURPOSE OF THIS BOOK

The more you learn about yourself, the better able you are to wisely use the energies in your life. For more than 3,000 years, astrology has been the sharpest tool in the box for describing the human condition. Used by virtually every culture on the planet, astrology continues to serve as a link between individual lives and planetary cycles. We gain valuable insights into personal issues with a birth chart, and can plot the patterns of the year ahead in meaningful ways for individuals as well as groups. You share your sun sign with eight percent of humanity. Clearly, you're not all going to have the same day, even if the basic astrological cycles are the same. Your individual circumstances, the specific factors of your entire birth chart, and your own free will help you write your unique story.

The purpose of this book is to describe the energies of the Sun, Moon, and planets for the year ahead and help you create your future, rather than being a victim of it. We aim to facilitate your journey by showing you the turns ahead in the road of life and hopefully the best ways to navigate them.

YOU ARE THE STAR OF YOUR LIFE

It is not our goal to simply predict events. Rather, we are reporting the planetary energies—the cosmic weather in which you are living—so that you understand these conditions and know how to use them most effectively.

The power, though, isn't in the stars, but in your mind, your heart, and the choices that you make every day. Regardless of how strongly you are buffeted by the winds of change or bored by stagnation, you have many ways to view any situation. Learning about the energies of the Sun, Moon, and planets will both sharpen and widen your perspective, thereby giving you additional choices.

The language of astrology is a gift of awareness, not a rigid set of rules. It works best when blended with common sense, intuition, and self-trust. This is your life, and no one knows how to live it as well as you. Take what you need from this book and leave the rest. Although the planets set the stage for the year ahead, you're the writer, director, and star of your life and you can play the part in whatever way you choose. *Your Personal Astrology Planner* uses information about your sun sign to give you a better understanding of how the planetary waves will wash upon your shore. We each navigate our lives through time, and each moment has unique qualities. Astrology gives us the ability to describe the constantly changing timescape. For example, if you know the trajectory and the speed of an approaching storm, you can choose to delay a leisurely afternoon sail on the bay, thus avoiding an unpleasant situation.

By reading this book, you can improve your ability to align with the cosmic weather, the larger patterns that affect you day to day. You can become more effective by aligning with the cosmos and cocreating the year ahead with a better understanding of the energies around you.

Astrology doesn't provide quick fixes to life's complex issues. It doesn't offer neatly packed black-and-white answers in a world filled with an infinite variety of shapes and colors. It can, however, give you a much clearer picture of the invisible forces influencing your life.

ENERGY & EVENTS

Two sailboats can face the same gale yet travel in opposite directions as a result of how the sails are positioned. Similarly, how you respond to the energy of a particular set of circumstances may be more responsible for your fate than the given situation itself. We delineate the energetic winds for your year ahead, but your attitude shapes the unfolding events, and your responses alter your destiny.

This book emphasizes the positive, not because all is good, but because astrology shows us ways to transform even the power of a storm into beneficial results. Empowerment comes from learning to see the invisible energy patterns that impact the visible landscape as you fill in the details of your story every day on this spinning planet, orbited by the Moon, lit by the Sun, and colored by the nuances of the planets.

You are a unique point in an infinite galaxy of unlimited possibilities, and the choices that you make have consequences. So use this book in a most magical way to consciously improve your life.

MOON CHARTS

2008 NEW MOONS

Each New Moon marks the beginning of a cycle. In general, this is the best time to plant seeds for future growth. Use the days preceeding the New Moon to finish old business prior to starting what comes next. The focused mind can be quite sharp during this phase. Harness the potential of the New Moon by stating your intentions—out loud or in writing—for the weeks ahead. Hold these goals in your mind; help them grow to fruition through conscious actions as the Moon gains light during the following two weeks. In the chart below, the dates and times refer to when the Moon and Sun align in each zodiac sign (see p16), initiating a new lunar cycle.

DATE	TIME	SIGN
January 8	6:37 AM EST	Capricorn
February 6	10:43 PM EST	Aquarius **(ECLIPSE)**
March 7	12:13 PM EST	Pisces
April 5	11:54 PM EDT	Aries
May 5	8:18 AM EDT	Taurus
June 3	3:22 PM EDT	Gemini
July 2	10:19 PM EDT	Cancer
August 1	6:12 AM EDT	Leo **(ECLIPSE)**
August 30	3:58 PM EDT	Virgo
September 29	4:12 AM EDT	Libra
October 28	7:14 PM EDT	Scorpio
November 27	11:54 AM EST	Sagittarius
December 27	7:22 AM EST	Capricorn

2008 FULL MOONS

The Full Moon reflects the light of the Sun as subjective feelings reflect the objective events of the day. Dreams seem bigger; moods feel stronger. The emotional waters run with deeper currents. This is the phase of culmination, a turning point in the energetic cycle. Now it's time to listen to the inner voices. Rather than starting new projects, the two weeks after the Full Moon are when we complete what we can and slow our outward expressions in anticipation of the next New Moon. In this chart, the dates and times refer to when the moon is opposite the sun in each zodiac sign, marking the emotional peak of each lunar cycle.

DATE	TIME	SIGN
January 22	8:35 AM EST	Leo
February 20	10:31 PM EST	Virgo **(ECLIPSE)**
March 21	2:40 PM EDT	Libra
April 20	6:25 AM EDT	Scorpio
May 19	10:11 PM EDT	Scorpio
June 18	1:30 PM EDT	Sagittarius
July 18	3:58 AM EDT	Capricorn
August 16	5:16 PM EDT	Aquarius **(ECLIPSE)**
September 15	5:13 AM EDT	Pisces
October 14	4:01 PM EDT	Aries
November 13	1:16 AM EST	Taurus
December 12	11:37 AM EST	Gemini

ASTROLOGY, YOU & THE WORLD

WELCOME TO YOUR SUN SIGN

The Sun, Moon, and Earth and all the planets lie within a plane called the **ecliptic** and move through a narrow band of stars made up by 12 constellations called the **zodiac**. The Earth revolves around the Sun once a year, but from our point of view, it appears that the Sun moves through each sign of the zodiac for one month. There are 12 months and astrologically there are 12 signs. The astrological months, however, do not match our calendar, and start between the 19th and 23rd of each month. Everyone is born to an astrological month, like being born in a room with a particular perspective of the world. Knowing your sun sign provides useful information about your personality and your future, but for a more detailed astrological analysis, a full birth chart calculation based on your precise date, time, and place of birth is necessary. Get your complete birth chart online at:

http://www.tarot.com/astrology/astroprofile

This book is about your zodiac sign. Your Sun is in spiritual and intuitive Pisces, a water sign that knows no boundaries. The encompassing nature of your being makes you compassionate and idealistic, but it also requires you to pull away from others when they wear you out or drown out your own thoughts and feelings. Take advantage of any private time you get, since it's a chance to explore your incredible imagination and creative ability.

THE PLANETS

We refer to the Sun and Moon as planets. Don't worry; we do know about modern astronomy. Although the Sun is really a star and the Moon is a satellite, they are called planets for astrological purposes. The astrological planets are the Sun, the Moon, Mercury, Venus, Mars, Jupiter, Saturn, Chiron, Uranus, Neptune, and Pluto.

Your sun sign is the most obvious astrological placement, for the Sun returns to the same sign every year. But at the same time, the Moon is orbiting the Earth, changing signs every two and a third days. Mercury, Venus, and Mars each move through a sign in a few weeks to a few months.

Jupiter spends a whole year in a sign—and Pluto visits a sign for up to 30 years! The ever-changing positions of the planets alter the energetic terrain through which we travel. The planets are symbols; each has a particular range of meanings. For example, Venus is the goddess of love, but it really symbolizes beauty in a spectrum of experiences. Venus can represent romantic love, sensuality, the arts, or good food. It activates anything that we value, including personal possessions and even money. To our ancestors, the planets actually animated life on Earth. In this way of thinking, every beautiful flower contains the essence of Venus.

Each sign has a natural affinity to an individual planet, and as this planet moves through the sky, it sends messages of particular interest to people born under that sign. Jupiter, your traditional key or ruling planet, raises hopes, motivates you to take chances, and demonstrates your generosity. Neptune, the modern ruler of Pisces, erases the boundaries between dreams and reality, which can bring confusion but often fills you with inspiration. Planets can be described by many different words, for the mythology of each is a rich tapestry. In this book we use a variety of words when talking about each planet in order to convey the most applicable meaning. The table below describes a few keywords for each planet, including the Sun and Moon.

PLANET	SYMBOL	KEYWORDS
Sun	☉	Consciousness, Will, Vitality
Moon	☽	Subconscious, Emotions, Habits
Mercury	☿	Communication, Thoughts, Transportation
Venus	♀	Desire, Love, Money, Values
Mars	♂	Action, Physical Energy, Drive
Jupiter	♃	Expansion, Growth, Optimism
Saturn	♄	Contraction, Maturity, Responsibility
Chiron	⚷	Healing, Pain, Subversion
Uranus	♅	Awakening, Unpredictable, Inventive
Neptune	♆	Imagination, Spirituality, Confusion
Pluto	♇	Passion, Intensity, Regeneration

HOUSES

Just as planets move through the signs of the zodiac, they also move through the houses in an individual chart. The 12 houses correspond to the 12 signs, but are individualized, based upon your sign. In this book we use Solar Houses, which place your sun sign in your 1st House. Therefore, when a planet enters a new sign it also enters a new house. If you know your exact time of birth, the rising sign determines the 1st House. You can learn your rising sign by entering your birth date at:

http://www.tarot.com/astrology/astroprofile

HOUSE	SIGN	KEYWORDS
1st House	Aries	Self, Appearance, Personality
2nd House	Taurus	Possessions, Values, Self-Worth
3rd House	Gemini	Communication, Siblings, Short Trips
4th House	Cancer	Home, Family, Roots
5th House	Leo	Love, Romance, Children, Play
6th House	Virgo	Work, Health, Daily Routines
7th House	Libra	Marriage, Relationships, Business Partners
8th House	Scorpio	Intimacy, Transformation, Shared Resources
9th House	Sagittarius	Travel, Higher Education, Philosophy
10th House	Capricorn	Career, Community, Ambition
11th House	Aquarius	Groups and Friends, Associations, Social Ideals
12th House	Pisces	Imagination, Spirituality, Secret Activities

ASPECTS

As the planets move through the sky in their various cycles, they form ever-changing angles with one another. Certain angles create significant geometric shapes. So, when two planets are 90 degrees apart, they conform to a square; 60 degrees of separation conforms to a sextile, or six-pointed star. Planets create **aspects** when they're at these special angles. Aspects explain how the individual symbolism of pairs of planets combine into an energetic pattern.

ASPECT	DEGREES	KEYWORDS
Conjunction	0	Compression, Blending, Focus
Opposition	180	Tension, Awareness, Balance
Trine	120	Harmony, Free-Flowing, Ease
Square	90	Resistance, Stress, Dynamic Conflict
Quintile	72	Creativity, Metaphysical, Magic
Sextile	60	Support, Intelligent, Activating
Quincunx	150	Irritation, Annoyance, Adjustment

2008 GENERAL FORECAST:
THE INDIVIDUAL AND THE COLLECTIVE

Astrology works for individuals, groups, and even humanity as a whole. You will have your own story in 2008, but it will unfold among 6.7 billion other tales of human experience. We are each unique, yet our lives touch one another; our destinies are woven together by weather and war, by economy, science, politics, religion, and all the other threads of life on this planet. We make personal choices every day, yet there are great events beyond the control of any one individual. When the power goes out in a neighborhood, it affects everyone, yet individual astrology patterns will describe the personal response of each person.

We are living at a time when the tools of self-awareness fill bookshelves, Web sites, and broadcasts, and we benefit greatly from them. Yet despite all this wisdom, conflicts among groups cause enormous suffering. Understanding personal issues is a powerful means for increasing happiness, but knowledge of our collective issues is equally important for our well-being. This forecast of the major trends and planetary patterns for 2008 provides a framework for understanding the potentials and challenges we face together, so that we can advance with tolerance and respect as a community and fulfill our potentials as individuals.

The astrological events used for this forecast are the transits of major planets Jupiter and Saturn, the retrograde cycles of Mercury, and the eclipses of the Sun and the Moon.

A NOTE ABOUT THE DATES IN THIS BOOK

All events are based upon the Eastern Time Zone of the United States. Because of local time differences, an event occurring just minutes after midnight in the East will actually happen the prior day in the rest of the country. Although the key dates are the exact dates of any particular alignment, some of you are so ready for certain things to happen that you can react to a transit a day or two before it is exact. And sometimes you could be so entrenched in habits or unwilling to change that you may not notice the effects right away. Allow extra time around each key date to feel the impact of any event.

JUPITER IN CAPRICORN

MATERIALIZING SUCCESS

December 18, 2007–January 5, 2009

Optimistic Jupiter is ready to climb a mountain this year. Instead of simply heading off on an adventure, the planet of expansion's passage through industrious Capricorn is a time to set goals, plan a course of action, and reach the summit of success. Jolly Jupiter is usually happy exploring the world, seeking new experiences, and expanding the mind. But Saturn-ruled Capricorn puts the giant planet in a productive mood where the name of the game is getting results. Opportunities come for those who do their homework and demonstrate the patience and commitment to prove their worthiness. There's less room for sloppiness for those who want chance to turn in their favor. Good luck is earned only by solid effort this year.

Jupiter in Capricorn is a time to turn beliefs into reality. Idealistic philosophies lose their meaning unless practice brings them down to earth. The enormous planet loves the biggest ideas, but Capricorn's practicality will test them against the weight of experience. The dark side of Jupiter's presence here is materialism that values worldly achievement more than spiritual awakening. Instead of living up to standards that may be difficult to reach, it will be tempting to lower those standards or just do away with them entirely.

Hope for a balanced approach to ambition occurs with positive trines between Jupiter and Saturn in January, September, and November. These healthy alignments between the planets of expansion and contraction bring the wisdom of self-restraint and a willingness to earn one's rewards honestly. Those who play by the rules should get what they deserve, while those who cut corners are likely to slide right off the track and slip farther from their aspirations. The Jupiter-Saturn trine in earth signs adds conscientiousness and a capacity to put in the time necessary to attain one's goals.

Positive 60-degree sextiles between Jupiter and inventive Uranus in late March, May, and November supply a plethora of fresh ideas that help us avoid repeating old mistakes. The pragmatism of Jupiter and Saturn in earth signs has a conservative side that would normally resist untested concepts. But Uranus's aspects with Jupiter weave intuition into the year's fabric to brighten it with originality. Jupiter's friendly relationships with the planets of the old tried and true (Saturn) and new and untested (Uranus) combines the best of the past and the future.

SATURN IN VIRGO
MANAGING THE DETAILS
September 2, 2007–October 29, 2009

Saturn, the planet of boundaries and limitations, takes twenty-nine years to orbit the Sun and pass through all twelve signs of the zodiac. It demands serious responsibility, shows the work needed to overcome obstacles, and teaches us how to build new structures in our lives. Saturn thrives on patience and commitment, rewarding well-planned and persistent effort but punishing sloppiness with delay, disappointment, and failure.

Saturn's passage through detail-oriented Virgo is a time to perfect skills, cut waste, and develop healthier habits. Saturn and Virgo are both pragmatic, which makes them an excellent pair for improving the quality of material life. Organizational upgrades and maintenance projects increase efficiency for individuals and organizations. Education and training become more valuable due to the increasing demand for highly specialized skills. Carelessness grows more costly, because minor errors can escalate into major problems. Systems break down easily, requiring closer attention than usual. Bodies can be more susceptible to illnesses caused by impure food or water, making this an ideal time to improve your diet. Environmental issues grow in importance as we approach a critical point in the relationship between humanity and planet Earth. Fortunately, Saturn in exacting Virgo is excellent for cleaning up unhealthy toxins produced by old technologies and in leading the way to develop new ecologically friendly systems for the future.

Saturn in Virgo highlights flaws and makes it easier to be critical of oneself and others. Yet its true purpose is to solve problems, not simply complain about them. Recognizing our weaknesses can sometimes be a source of despair, but the functional combination of Saturn's commitment and Virgo's analytical skills gives hope that effective change is well within our grasp. Small steps in a positive direction can slowly build up to a tidal wave of improvement wherever you place your attention this year.

MERCURY RETROGRADES

January 28–February 18 in Aquarius / May 26–June 19 in Gemini / September 23–October 15 in Libra

All true planets appear to move retrograde from time to time as a result of viewing them from the moving platform of Earth. The most significant retrograde periods are those of Mercury, the communication planet. Occurring three times a year for roughly three weeks at a time, these are periods when difficulties with details, travel, information flow, and technical matters are likely.

Although Mercury's retrograde phase has received a fair amount of bad press, it isn't necessarily a negative cycle. Because personal and commercial interactions are emphasized, you can actually accomplish more than usual, especially if you stay focused on what needs to be done rather than initiating new projects. But you may feel as if you're treading water—or worse yet, being carried backward in an undertow of unfinished business. Worry less about making progress than about the quality of your work. Pay extra attention to your communication exchanges. Avoiding misunderstandings is the ideal way to preemptively deal with unnecessary complications. Retrograde Mercury is best used to tie up loose ends as you review, redo, reconsider, and, in general, revisit the past.

This year, the three retrogrades are in intellectual air signs (Aquarius, Gemini, and Libra), which can be very useful for analysis and remedial studies that help you reevaluate what you already know so you can take your learning to the next step. Mercury has a natural affinity for the air signs, so you are empowered by your mental prowess during these times. But however intelligent you feel, don't become so enamored with the workings of your mind that you forget about the practical aspects of your body and the emotional needs of your heart.

ECLIPSES

Solar: February 6 and August 1

Lunar: February 20 and August 16

Solar and Lunar Eclipses are special New and Full Moons that indicate meaningful changes for individuals and groups. They are powerful markers of events whose influences can appear up to three months in advance and last up to six months afterward.

February 6, Solar Eclipse in Aquarius: Community Concerns
A revolutionary point of view can put an end to old fantasies and give birth to new dreams as mental Mercury and idealistic Neptune join the Sun and Moon during this eclipse. Aquarius allows a wide-spectrum view in which we can see our individual lives within the larger context of teams, groups, and community. Chiron, the Wounded Healer, also joins the eclipse point, which can increase compassion globally, give birth to new social organizations, and stir more interest in charitable activities. Charismatic leaders may emerge with fresh ideas for reinvigorating society. But it could be difficult to

determine which are capable of bringing about real change and which are simply masters of illusion.

February 20, Lunar Eclipse in Virgo: Fix What's Broken
This total eclipse of the Moon in critical Virgo reveals flaws in current systems, regardless of how much effort was put into building them. Serious Saturn conjunct the Moon reflects the hard work invested in the physical and emotional structures that are starting to fail now. A Lunar Eclipse is about letting go of the past, but both the Moon and Saturn are resistant to change. Virgo's analytical abilities permit us to justify these outmoded patterns with reason and practicality. But the Pisces Sun in opposition shows that the creative path of faith and imagination will take us farther than roads of duty, obligation, and habit. When daily details drain the joy out of life, it's clear that change is necessary. Yet we may feel the need to choose between a reality that's not fully satisfying and a dream that we fear will never come true. Fortunately, evolutionary Pluto forms a creative 120-degree trine with the eclipse that eliminates nonessential tasks to free up time and energy for more meaningful activities.

August 1, Solar Eclipse in Leo: Creativity Shines
Eclipses of the Sun are often associated with the fall of leaders. This one in the Sun's own sign of Leo is visible through central Russia and China, where changes at the top are most likely to occur. On a personal level, Solar

Eclipses are reminders to tame the ego and to balance will with humility. At its best, Leo is a sign of creative expression and generosity, but at its worst it represents a petulant, demanding child. Oppositions to this Sun-Moon conjunction from Neptune and Chiron add vulnerability and engender the kind of insecurity that may provoke immature behavior. Expect drama, but don't allow it to take over. Instead of giving in to the demands of others or to your own fears, step back and permit the storm to pass. This eclipse can bring healing through self-acceptance and recognition that even the biggest stories are only chapters in the book of life.

August 16, Lunar Eclipse in Aquarius: Make New Friends
This partial Lunar Eclipse is joined with nebulous Neptune, which could bring floods and fraud into the headlines. Otherwise honorable organizations may be touched by scandal or exposed as severely underfunded. Individually, this eclipse is excellent for letting go of beliefs that don't correspond with your current reality. Outdated ideals or dreams may need to be discarded, which can be painful, but awakening to today's truth brings a breath of fresh air that clears clutter from the mind. Cooperation is the key with Aquarius, so recognizing where friends and allies are more hindrance than help is important.

Remember that all of these astrological events are part of the general cosmic weather for the year, but will affect us each differently based upon our individual astrological signs.

2008 HOROSCOPE

PISCES

FEBRUARY 19–MARCH 20

OVERVIEW OF THE YEAR

You can reach new levels of fulfillment this year when you participate as part of a team, because optimistic Jupiter, your co-ruling planet, is in your 11th House of Groups. Opportunities to advance professionally depend on the support of colleagues and your ability to network professionally. **You're ready for more responsibility and higher achievement, but ultimately your success depends on the quality of relationships you create with others.** Serious Saturn is in your 7th House of Partnerships now, making your closest alliances the most challenging area of your life. Your tender heart hates to reject or criticize people, yet it's vital to associate yourself with those who are dedicated, competent, and willing to work as hard as you do. **Carrying the load of a less-than-capable partner can wear you down in your personal life or hold you back in your career**. Fortunately, Jupiter and Saturn form three harmonious trines this year that help you discover a balance between being compassionate and setting limits. These giant planets align on January 21,

September 8, and November 21 in the practical earth signs of Capricorn and Virgo to connect your lofty ambitions for tomorrow with the reality of today. Establishing well-defined goals and creating a strategy to achieve them is well within your reach.

Your other key planet is Neptune, and this year it will underscore your innate spiritual inclination as it continues the long journey through your 12th House of Soul Consciousness that began in 1999. **Two eclipses in the 12th House, though, turn this into a critical year of letting go of old metaphysical concepts and religious beliefs, preparing you for new dimensions of awareness.** The Solar Eclipse on February 6 is conjunct diffusive Neptune, carrying waves of feeling that are overwhelming even to you. Yet if you can just let go and ride them with faith, they will bring you to a place of deep wisdom and inspiration. The Lunar Eclipse on August 16 is as powerful as an inner tsunami that pulls you far from familiar territory. You could easily feel lost and anxious to return your feet to solid ground. But when you are willing to release the past and fully embrace the present, old wounds and doubts are washed away and the world becomes fresh and new again.

Visionary Neptune can supply another magical moment when it conjuncts the karmic North Node of the Moon on May 2, with rippling effects throughout the year. **This rare meeting is one more reminder of the spiritual freedom that can be yours now.** You may attract a teacher or companion who touches your soul and helps you overcome any sense of separation you have with others and the world around you. If you're already advanced on a path of personal awakening, you might become a source of inspiration for those seeking enlightenment. Take time out from your worldly ambitions and responsibilities to fill yourself with the spirit that can be found in nature, music, yoga, or meditation. The benefits may not appear on your résumé or bank statement, but they are precious nonetheless.

TAKE CHARGE

Authoritative Saturn's transit through your 7th House of Partnerships signals a need to take a stronger stance in relationships. Know what you want from others, be willing to state it, and then back it up with action. If you don't follow these critical steps, you won't experience the quality of companionship you deserve. A Lunar Eclipse on February 20 in your 7th House could mark a significant turning point in relationships. A near opposition between aggressive Mars and passionate Pluto can precipitate a point of no return where a situation must change or end. Happily, Pluto forms a supportive trine to the Moon that can direct difficult emotions toward a productive discussion, possibly transforming a painful partnership into a fulfilling one. If you're single, don't be afraid of your feelings. Even if they lead you to a place of hopelessness, don't give up. When you stay open to your heart, the intensity of your emotions can lead to a breakthrough—removing the barriers blocking you from the intimacy you desire.

CREATIVE OPPORTUNITIES

The supportive trine between hopeful Jupiter, the ruler of your 10th House of Career, and realistic Saturn provides a stable base for your advancement this year. You will be able to separate professional issues from personal ones with this highly practical pair working on your behalf. However, the Solar Eclipse in your 6th House of Employment on August 1 has long-lasting effects that could spur you to take creative risks on the job. Ideally, it encourages you to be bolder, express yourself more fully, and put more of your heart into daily life. Rather than simply accepting a humdrum routine, you may take chances by seeking new employment, starting your own business, or demonstrating more leadership in your present position. This could ruffle the feathers of an insecure boss or colleague, so consider his or her feelings before taking action.

STEADY AS SHE GOES

Your financial picture is relatively solid this year—with two exceptions. The New Moon in impetuous Aries on April 5 lights up your 2nd House of Resources to encourage spending. Spontaneous Mars, the ruler of this house, forms a tense square to the New Moon, as does expansive Jupiter. While you may long to spend your money on short-term fun, you'd be better off investing in training or equipment that increases your potential for long-term income. Also, be especially careful about borrowing or lending money from September 24–October 15, when logical Mercury loses its bearings while moving retrograde through your 8th House of Shared Resources.

ALTERNATIVE HEALTH

Inventive Uranus transiting your 1st House of Physicality picks up dynamic sextiles from adventurous Jupiter on March 28, May 21, and November 13 that can generate sudden changes of habit. New forms of exercise or an unconventional diet could reshape your body and boost your energy levels. Use your intuitive understanding of what's naturally healthy to make positive choices based on your own instincts rather than relying so much on the judgment of others.

SETTING LIMITS

Additional responsibilities for relatives or close friends can cramp your style at home this year. If you do have to bear a heavier burden of care for others, try to set clear boundaries about what you will or won't do to avoid being drained by endless demands. This is especially important May 26–June 19, when communicative Mercury marches backward through your 4th House of Home and Family and the chances for misunderstanding increase. Avoid any major changes to your residence during these weeks, too, unless they're for emergency repairs.

MIX PLEASURE WITH BUSINESS

Short trips for practical purposes can be very productive for you this year. Keep your agenda well defined so you can take care of business without sacrificing time off for fun. Group travel can be rewarding, but it's almost certain to entail complications. Work out all the details in advance to reduce the number of snags you're likely to encounter. Educational pursuits work best when you have a specific goal in mind. Gaining certification or a degree to advance your career makes good sense, but aiming for a master's degree in art history because you love art probably isn't a wise investment.

SIXTH SENSE

Pisces has a closer connection to the spiritual dimension and dream world than any other sign, and this is an excellent year to put your awareness into practice. You are no longer a novice, but can act as a direct channel for soul-centered information. Your planet Neptune nurtures your intuition, so trust it every chance you get. Even if your interpretations are off from time to time, continue to use your psychic powers—your accuracy will improve. If there are moments when your faith flags, see what you can do to help someone in need. When you give to others, your compassion lifts you above your own doubts and fears and quickly returns you to your center.

RICK & JEFF'S TIP FOR THE YEAR

Find Your Center

Your idealism makes it all too easy to experience extreme ups and downs. The search for the divine, for the perfect romance, for the most sublime experiences takes you to places few people ever go—which is why the fall can be so hard when these journeys end. This is a year to temper those highs and lows by finding beauty in the little things and delight in your daily life. This is not meant to limit your emotional range, but to widen your center so that satisfaction is never beyond your reach. The greatest joys of the universe exist as much within you as anywhere else.

JANUARY

LIGHTEN YOUR LOAD

The year starts with energetic Mars moving retrograde in your 10th House of Career, leaving you backpedaling professionally or feeling overloaded with unfinished chores. This isn't the best time to take on additional responsibilities, even if you enjoy juggling several tasks at a time. An intense opposition between Mars and penetrating Pluto on **January 2** requires all the concentration you can muster to deal with demanding issues at home or on the job. The New Moon in orderly Capricorn on **January 8**, though, falls in your 11th House of Groups and could bring much-appreciated assistance from friends or colleagues. It's a signal for you to act as a leader and organize team efforts instead of carrying the ball by yourself. On **January 21**, your traditional ruling planet Jupiter forms the first of three constructive trines with responsible Saturn, a pattern that will repeat on **September 8 and November 21**. This cooperative alignment between the planets of hope and reality helps you establish strategic plans for reaching your long-term goals.

The Full Moon in dramatic Leo on **January 22** sparks creativity that can be applied to your job or a hobby. Pluto enters ambitious Capricorn and your 11th House on **January 25**, beginning a lengthy process of transition in your role within groups or in community work. Thoughtful Mercury turns retrograde on **January 28** to kick off a three-week review of spiritual values and personal dreams. Take extra care in communication to avoid misunderstandings during this detail-challenged period. You may feel the urge to initiate a project when dynamic Mars turns direct on **January 30**. Its forward movement greases the wheels of activity, but it's best to avoid major moves until Mercury also goes direct on **February 18**.

KEEP IN MIND THIS MONTH

It's flattering to be offered a leadership position, but carefully consider the additional demands on your time and energy before accepting.

KEY DATES

★ **JANUARY 6–8**

foot in mouth

A clever quintile between loving Venus and whimsical Neptune on **January 6** can turn an ordinary day into one inspired by new forms of pleasure, romance, and delight. Mercury enters intelligent Aquarius and your 12th House of Soul Consciousness on **January 7**, strengthening your natural intuition. A taut semisquare between Mercury and eccentric Uranus on **January 8** may have surprising ideas popping into your head and out of your mouth. Yet with the New Moon in strict Capricorn, you could be held accountable for every word you say. If you do stumble verbally, correct yourself quickly, apologize, and move on.

★ **JANUARY 12**

keep the faith

Your two ruling planets, visionary Jupiter and spiritual Neptune, cross paths in a semisquare that can blur your judgment with boundless hope. Overlooking details is to be expected, but this planetary pair might infuse you with faith in something larger than yourself, lifting your spirits and reducing the stress of daily life.

★ JANUARY 16
compassionate heart

An awkward quincunx between the willful Sun and impatient Mars can waste your energy or cause an inadvertent clash with a family member or colleague. But any wounded feelings will quickly heal, because you can respond graciously with a lovely sextile between diplomatic Venus and forgiving Neptune. Your natural instinct to see the best in others makes it easy to dismiss their faults and appreciate their talents. A touch of artistry adds romance and beauty, even in the midst of a challenging task.

SUPER NOVA DAYS

★ JANUARY 20–22
secret support

The Sun's entry into unconventional Aquarius on **January 20** shines light in your 12th House of Divinity, where it warms your soul and heightens your psychic powers. Help can come your way from unexpected sources, while the energy you have to offer those in need continues to grow. On **January 21**, a trine between Jupiter and Saturn, the cosmic regulators, rocks you in a big cradle of security. You know that you can take your time getting where you want to go in life because you're already on the right track. Retrograde Mercury conjuncts nebulous Neptune on **January 22**, turning ordinary reality into a magical world where imagination flourishes but facts and details may get fuzzy.

★ JANUARY 28–30
dazed and confused

Like ships passing in the night, talkative Mercury turns retrograde on **January 28** and assertive Mars goes direct on **January 30**. In between, a vulnerable Venus-Neptune semisquare on **January 29** can leave you feeling lost with all these planetary comings and goings. Seeking escape via careless spending or romantic fantasies is a short-term fix with the potential for long-term problems, so keep your diversions simple.

FEBRUARY

RELATIONSHIP REALITY

This is a dynamic month highlighted by two eclipses, Mercury turning direct, and the Sun entering imaginative Pisces. The Solar Eclipse on **February 6** in unorthodox Aquarius falls in your 12th House of Destiny and can have a profound impact on your most cherished spiritual beliefs. Its conjunction with your ruling planet Neptune makes you feel as if a curtain has opened, allowing you to peer into a magical new world. The vision you see has the potential to touch your soul and inspire you for years to come. Unfortunately, it might be difficult to describe this experience to others. In fact, quietly nurturing the flame you feel inside is the best way to ensure its continuation: Too much conversation can dissipate its intuitive power. Mercury stops dead in its tracks on **February 18** and slowly begins moving direct again after its three-week retrograde cycle. This forward shift of the communication planet frees up data that's been lost in translation and reveals messages hidden in the bottom of your e-mail box. Mercury's turnaround in your 12th House of

Spirituality continues this month's trend of opening your awareness to other levels of consciousness.

The Sun's entry into your inspirational sign on **February 19** feeds your creativity and boosts your self-confidence. You know how to push ahead with sensitivity to advance your interests while avoiding friction. A Lunar Eclipse in critical Virgo on **February 20** is likely to result in a thorough reevaluation of relationships. Its conjunction with limit-setting Saturn in your 7th House of Partnerships shows that the time has come to clarify where you stand with others. Commit to those who are willing to work with you and kindly cut loose those who aren't.

KEEP IN MIND THIS MONTH

Shifting your mind from the boundless world of spirit to the limits of relationship requires a flexible attitude and a strong sense of realism.

KEY DATES

★ **FEBRUARY 1–2**

sweet distraction

A juicy conjunction between sociable Venus and jovial Jupiter on **February 1** almost guarantees you pleasant company. The planets' union in your 11th House of Groups shows off your ability to organize and entertain for a perfect mix of business and pleasure. Retrograde Mercury backs over fanciful Neptune on **February 2**, which is wonderful for intimate conversations and spiritual connections, but facts get fuzzy and messages are easily misplaced or misunderstood. Double-check details to avoid mix-ups.

★ **FEBRUARY 6**

save yourself

Mental Mercury joins the Sun during today's electric Aquarius Solar Eclipse, and offers an unexpected chance for introspection—reawakening memories that have been buried for years. Pay attention to your dreams, because they are a rich source of information that can help you make sense out of your past and put you on a clear path to the future. An individual you idealize may take a fall in your eyes. The message is that you don't need any heroes to show you the way; you have all the inspiration and power you need within yourself.

★ FEBRUARY 10

lost in wonderland

The annual conjunction between the Sun and Neptune carries you beyond the bounds of the mundane. This could be a trip to fantasyland that winds up distracting you from reality. Yet you could also experience a sense of connection that erases barriers, washes away criticism, and reminds you of the divinity in all things. However, you're going to have to live with the choices you make when you come off this cloud, so avoid making promises you can't keep.

SUPER NOVA DAYS

★ FEBRUARY 17–20

narrow your focus

An overly optimistic semisquare between the Sun and excessive Jupiter can prove overwhelming if you make too many social commitments on **February 17**. Intellectual Mercury's direct turn on **February 18**, though, can get you back on track mentally as your thinking and communication sharpen. The Sun's entry into sweet and sensitive Pisces on **February 19** is buttressed by a supportive sextile with Pluto. Your sign's faith is channeled by deep perceptions that show you where to focus and where to let go. The Lunar Eclipse on **February 20** in practical Virgo, joined with no-nonsense Saturn, demands complete concentration and shuts down your efforts where there's nothing to be gained.

★ **FEBRUARY 24**
relationship test
The Sun's opposition with Saturn is a reality check for your relationships. You may reach the end of the road with one person, recognizing that you may never get what you desire. But it can also solidify partnerships when you share the same goals and are willing to put in an equal amount of work to reach them.

MARCH

STORMY WEATHER

Impulsive Mars enters watery Cancer and your 5th House of Romance and Self-Expression on **March 4**, making this a time to act on your feelings. It's your turn to take the initiative in matters of the heart and to demonstrate your creativity. You often wear your emotions on your sleeve, yet you're now able to direct them with a sense of purpose, making you more attractive to others. Staying calm, however, can be tough this month with the sensitive Pisces New Moon closely conjunct shocking Uranus on **March 7**. The presence of astrology's most rebellious planet at the annual union of the Sun and Moon in your sign indicates that you're in a very dynamic period of change—one that might generate dramatic events and strong reactions without warning. You can apply this revolutionary force productively by letting go of outmoded habits and actively engaging in new and unconventional experiences.

Creative Venus and intellectual Mercury enter spiritual Pisces on **March 12 and March 14**, respectively. The presence of these fast-moving personal planets in your sign adds magic, imagination, and idealism to your life. Yet the high hopes they engender may loosen your grip on reality enough to lead you to some careless decisions. There's no limit to how far your mind or heart can travel, but keeping one foot solidly on the ground will keep you from floating off into dreamland. You may encounter a bump in the road when restricting Saturn forms a tense sesquisquare with encouraging Jupiter on **March 18**. Adjusting long-range plans now will help you solidify your future when this aspect returns again on **June 26 and January 30, 2009**.

KEEP IN MIND THIS MONTH

Stay loose in your thinking and fast on your feet to keep up with the rapid pace of change in your life.

KEY DATES

SUPER NOVA DAYS

★ **MARCH 6–9**

lightning strikes

A smart sextile between the Sun and wise Jupiter brings an optimistic perspective on **March 6**. A romantic Venus-Neptune conjunction only enhances this upbeat mood, painting the world in heartwarming colors . . . yet also blurring your judgment. The mood shifts radically on **March 7**, when a contentious opposition between aggressive Mars and unyielding Pluto brings emotions to a peak. The day's New Moon in Pisces joined with Uranus shakes your world with unexpected events, but can also excite you with the prospect of new discoveries and more freedom. The Sun's exact conjunction with electric Uranus on **March 8** keeps the buzz going, yet might also foster rebellion against an authority figure. Mental Mercury joins Neptune on **March 9**, allowing for more sensitive conversations but also enabling fantasy to carry your thinking far from reality.

★ MARCH 12–15

waking from a dream

Sweet Venus enters gentle Pisces on **March 12**, making you more alluring as you tune in to your own special gifts. Then, on **March 13**, a strengthening Venus-Pluto sextile tempers this delicate and idealistic transit, giving you clarity about your deep desires. A practical Mars-Saturn sextile on **March 14** helps you work productively with others and solidify ideas spawned by Mercury's entry into visionary Pisces. Relationships and self-worth may fluctuate considerably on **March 15**, when romantic Venus goes too far with a semisquare to Jupiter and is then deflated by a corrective opposition from serious Saturn.

★ MARCH 20–21

let go to grow

The Sun enters go-getter Aries and your 2nd House of Resources on **March 20** to mark the Vernal Equinox. The fiery force of the spring season can prompt money-making ideas and energize the process of increasing your income. The creative Sun's square to purging

Pluto on **March 21**, however, shows a need to cut back or reallocate expenses of cash or energy. If you face doubt or get caught up in a power struggle, letting go will work better than settling in for a long fight.

★ **MARCH 26–28**

high-frequency buzz

A mushy Mars-Neptune sesquisquare on **March 26** may push your efforts off target and waste your time unless you concentrate on what you're doing. Mental activity is running high on **March 27**, when Mercury conjuncts Uranus and sextiles Jupiter one day before these outer planets sextile each other. Brilliant ideas pop into your head so quickly, it may be difficult to describe them. Your nervous system could be overstimulated, so take time to relax and breathe if you get too wound up. Sexy Venus sextiles Jupiter and conjuncts Uranus on **March 28**, adding chills and thrills to your social life.

APRIL

MONEY ON YOUR MIND

A fresh look at finances is the key issue this month as the Sun continues to move through your 2nd House of Resources until **April 19**, picking up the company of brainy Mercury and charming Venus on **April 2 and April 6**. The presence of these planets in the pioneering sign of Aries reminds you how innovative you can be when it comes to money matters. The New Moon in spontaneous Aries on **April 5** can trigger a daring move, especially when dynamic squares from pushy Mars and enterprising Jupiter add their ambitious energies. A serious investment in a new venture can be the right choice if it has the potential to change how you earn your income. Boldly creating a business or expanding an existing one makes more sense than spending recklessly for your own pleasure.

The tone shifts on **April 17** when Mercury enters stable Taurus in your 3rd House of Information, followed by the Sun on **April 19**. If you slow down to clear your thinking and simplify your communication, you'll increase your credibility and earn more trust from others. Your imaginative mind is ready to come down to earth and absorb practical data, which makes you a more receptive student. The Full Moon in passionate Scorpio on **April 20** illuminates your 9th House of Philosophy and Religion, stimulating feelings of political or religious fervor. Powerful emotions provoke you to share your opinions with greater force than usual. Still, you'll likely have all the facts you need to back up these statements thanks to responsible Saturn in detail-oriented Virgo's supportive sextile to the Full Moon. You can apply what you now know to successfully build on any recent investments.

KEEP IN MIND THIS MONTH

Spend more time and energy on yourself: Focusing on your own needs now will pay dividends in the long run.

KEY DATES

★ **APRIL 5–7**

calculate the risks

The rowdy Aries New Moon on **April 5** can lead to leaping without looking, especially with pleasure-seeking Venus entering this fast-moving fire on **April 6**. However, Venus then forms a demanding square with exacting Pluto that will drive up the cost of careless spending. A forgiving semisquare between Mercury and Neptune on **April 7** can produce soft words, but there is no room for sloppy thinking as constricting Saturn makes a tough quincunx with Venus that can keep a relationship on edge.

★ **APRIL 10**

with a grain of salt

Beware of an overly expansive square between boundless Jupiter and the motivating Sun that encourages you to make promises too big to be kept. Confidence is warranted, but show some restraint to avoid overindulging or saying more than you should. Even a reliable friend or colleague can stretch the truth, so take what you hear with a dash of skepticism.

SUPER NOVA DAYS

★ APRIL 13–14

hope floats

Idealism rises on **April 13** with a Sun-Neptune sextile, yet you could definitely go overboard. A Venus-Neptune semisquare tends to overlook reality for a more romantic view of life, while a tense square from opinionated Jupiter to Mercury is prone to exaggeration. Filter through all the ideas around you to focus on the few that have immediate value. Serious Saturn hooks up with active Mars in a semisquare on **April 14**, narrowing your choices and requiring a more concentrated effort. A sensitive Mercury-Neptune sextile instigates inspiring conversations, but you need to take care of business before letting your mind wander.

★ APRIL 23–24

more, more, more

A sassy Venus-Mars square on **April 23** makes you extra creative in your pursuit of pleasure.

This talented but teasing pair's saucy planetary dance is dramatized by an indulgent Venus-Jupiter square on **April 23** and a super-energized Mars-Jupiter opposition on **April 24**. It's hard to avoid spending or socializing to the nth degree. Ideally, you can explore new flavors of delight without taking in more than you can digest.

★ **APRIL 28–29**

altered states

A careless Mars-Neptune quincunx on **April 28** makes it easy to drift off course. Fortunately, a highly perceptive trine between sharp-eyed Mercury and visionary Jupiter quickly realigns your thinking and places you back on track. Your communication skills are on point as you master details without losing sight of the big picture. The story is very different on **April 29** when Mercury's square to cloudy Neptune fogs your vision and skews your judgment. Don't rush into making important decisions until you've had a chance to gather more data and study the issues carefully.

MAY

CROSSCURRENTS

Four planets shift direction this month to swirl the waters of change. Structuring Saturn turns forward on **May 2** after traveling backward all year. This stabilizing influence is especially helpful for strengthening your position in relationships. If you've been thinking about altering a current partnership or seeking a new one, this is a smart time to put those wheels in motion. But don't act too quickly, for lucky Jupiter turns retrograde on **May 9**. You can continue to accrue gains during its four-month backward cycle, but digest experiences in small bites rather than gulping them down so hungrily that you can't assimilate all their benefits. Visionary Jupiter's reversal is also a reminder that the truth you seek exists within you, so rely on your inner guidance more than external authorities. Both Neptune and Mercury go retrograde on **May 26**. Your key planets, Jupiter and Neptune, urge you to reexamine your faith and invite you to deepen your spiritual journey during their retrograde phases. Mercury's three-week reversal in your 10th House of Career calls for greater caution in all of your communications and handling details related to your professional or public responsibilities.

The determined Taurus New Moon **May 5** sows seeds of curiosity in your 3rd House of Information. A supportive trine from wise Jupiter in practical Capricorn focuses your attention on utilitarian subjects that will give your words more credibility. Your actions may turn more dramatic when Mars enters theatrical Leo in your 6th House of Work and Service on **May 9**. Yet just as this creative force gets rolling, Mars forms an awkward quincunx with dominating Pluto on **May 11**. This demands the elimination of unnecessary activities prior to the intense Scorpio Full Moon in your expansive 9th House of Big Ideas.

KEEP IN MIND THIS MONTH

Slow and steady will get you much farther than fast and erratic, so manage your time and energy wisely to find a pace you can sustain.

KEY DATES

★ **MAY 2–3**

only the facts

Chatty Mercury enters its airy home sign of Gemini on **May 2**, which normally sets your mind spinning with a bouquet of stimulating ideas. Unfortunately, the communication planet slams into a square with limiting Saturn and a quincunx with obstinate Pluto on **May 3** that can complicate a conversation. If you want to make a point while avoiding an argument, keep it simple, stick to the facts, and be prepared to back them up with proof.

★ **MAY 7**

mind stretch

Mercury, the planet of details, clashes with Jupiter, the planet of big ideas, in a stressful sesquisquare. Under this aspect, exaggeration and overstatement can turn minor issues into major ones. Yet this can also be a chance to stretch yourself by processing complicated concepts or discussions—as long as you can distinguish the difference between facts and opinions.

★ **MAY 12–14**

be true to your heart

Your creative powers blossom on **May 12** when the Sun connects favorably to inventive Uranus and abundant Jupiter. Even if you've been knocked down recently, these energetic aspects give you the originality to find a fresh perspective and the confidence to express yourself. A square between the self-conscious Sun and sensitive Neptune on **May 14**, however, is more vulnerable, and may leave you feeling unrecognized for your efforts. It's tempting to let these emotions fade, but if they involve an ongoing pattern in an important relationship, it's best to speak up now.

SUPER NOVA DAYS

★ **MAY 18–22**

a brilliant way out

A vivacious Venus-Jupiter trine on **May 18** brings you delightful help from your friends. But the passionate Scorpio Full Moon on **May 19** in your 9th House of Faraway Places increases your hunger for something more. A tense square from illusory Neptune stimulates visions of escape from the routine of your daily life. Within these fantasies, though, is a core idea worth your attention: Let go of the impossible dream and you'll find one that you can make real. The Sun's entry into fickle Gemini on **May 20** usually brings distractions, but its stressful quincunx with Pluto on **May 21** demands that you deal with a persistent question of control. At the same time, a genius Jupiter-Uranus sextile enlightens you with flashes of insight that arouse an itch for change. The Sun's tough square with stern Saturn on **May 22**, though, still holds you in check with inescapable responsibilities. Tension can build as these restraints contrast with an explosive Mars-Uranus sesquisquare. You might feel your only choices are fight or flight, but right now you're inventive enough to find a much more creative solution.

JUNE

EYE-OPENING EXPERIENCES

The New Moon in inquisitive Gemini on **June 3** falls in your 4th House of Home and Family, where it stimulates a desire to add more variety to your life. Flirty Venus and friendly Mercury join this lunation, along with a supportive sextile from outgoing Mars in Leo—offering creativity and connections that could make your personal life much more interesting. Bright ideas and encouragement from others push you forward, yet it's best to make changes slowly. Gemini's ruling planet, Mercury, is still retrograde, so promises are only possibilities and not commitments until the Messenger shifts into forward gear on **June 19**.

Transformative Pluto retrogrades back into truthful Sagittarius on **June 13** for one last visit before returning to Capricorn on **November 26**. This is likely to stir issues on the job front as it touches your 10th House of Career. The Full Moon in strident Sagittarius on **June 18** also occurs in this house; differences of opinion on the job may upset your equilibrium. The Archer's penchant for frankness takes on added punch with the Moon's conjunction to potent Pluto. Excitable Uranus's square to this Full Moon increases the intensity, possibly inciting extreme reactions. You may be ready to quit without notice—or even have the rug pulled out from under you. But this is also your chance to break unhealthy habits, clean up unfinished business, and allow yourself enough time to take a long look into the future. Sagittarius is a visionary sign that opens your eyes to a more magnanimous view of life. Simply coping with the crises of the moment may only delay the inevitable. It's wiser to start considering major professional changes now.

KEEP IN MIND THIS MONTH

Instead of immediately reacting to a shock and dissipating your emotional energy, keep stirring your feelings to fuel an even greater leap forward.

KEY DATES

★ **JUNE 3–4**

delightful diversions

The curious Gemini New Moon on **June 3** is filled with delightful distractions. Communications from close friends or family members who have been out of touch bring laughter and joy to the day. All this stimulation, though, can make it hard to focus, so tune out the extraneous noise if you have serious work to do. Fortunately, a sextile between the Sun and active Mars on **June 4** could make you clever enough to take care of business no matter how much fun you're having.

★ **JUNE 13–15**

forgive and forget

A skittish Sun-Uranus square kicks **June 13** off to a restless start, but uncertainty is calmed with a healing trine between Venus and Neptune. This compassionate planetary pair doesn't let weirdness get in the way of love. If you're feeling strange, look around and you'll find beauty that gives life meaning and reestablishes your connection with the earth. A Sun-Neptune trine on **June 14** continues the theme of forgiveness, which is crucial right now due to a contentious conjunction between Mars and the Moon's South Node that awakens conflict. The battle is probably over an old issue that's better forgotten than fought over. Still, feisty Mars's quincunx with overdoing Jupiter on **June 15** inhibits compromise. If you have extra energy, use it on a healthy outdoor adventure rather than in anger or spite.

SUPER NOVA DAYS

★ JUNE 18–20

tumultuous waters

Emotions escalate on **June 18** as sweet Venus opposes dark Pluto and then enters watery Cancer. If a partner is unresponsive, pushing harder may not help. It's clear that you need more satisfaction in love, but creating joy for yourself is the best way to attract what you want. An edgy Mars-Uranus quincunx brings impatience on **June 19** that may rush you to seek a quick solution. Yet impetuous acts are more likely to carry you off track than lead you where you want to go. Mercury turning direct can open new channels of communication, but then the prideful Sun follows Venus's path from Pluto to Cancer on **June 20**, intensifying feelings on the Summer Solstice. Cancer may be cuddly, but Pluto's presence suggests that something has got to go before you can feel safe again.

★ **JUNE 25–26**

foolish illusions

A fuzzy sesquisquare between Venus and Neptune on **June 25** puts fantasy ahead of reality when you're evaluating people or making purchases. The cost of excess becomes clear when strict Saturn sesquisquares lenient Jupiter on **June 26**—use prudence to temper runaway enthusiasm. Additionally, revolutionary Uranus turns retrograde, signaling that personal freedom primarily comes from within during the next five months.

JULY

TAKE THE LEAD

Relationships and interactions of all kinds heat up this month as assertive Mars enters your 7th House of Partnerships on **July 1**. This dynamic planet's presence in detail-oriented Virgo can attract as much criticism as passion, but don't allow yourself to be bullied by aggressive people. Stating your needs clearly reduces confusion and increases your chances for gaining cooperation in a peaceful fashion. Hope for love springs from the cozy Cancer New Moon in your 5th House of Romance on **July 2**. Tender feelings can make you shy, yet your sensitivity is an asset that makes you more appealing when you're willing to show it. Communicative Mercury's entry into your expressive 5th House on **July 10** opens the door to intimate conversations where the quality of connection is more important than the words themselves. Loving Venus enters outgoing Leo on **July 12**, bringing more joy to your work and daily routine as you find fun in the most ordinary activities.

The businesslike Capricorn Full Moon on **July 18** occurs in your 11th House of Groups and Friends, making it eminently clear how much is expected of you as a member of a team. A supportive sextile from ingenious Uranus to the Full Moon shows you ways to meet these responsibilities with more freedom and less stress. Perhaps most important is holding colleagues and pals accountable for their actions so that you don't have to carry more than your fair share of the load. The Sun and Mercury enter proud Leo and your 6th House of Work and Service on **July 22** and **July 26**, increasing your confidence and creativity on the job and empowering you to be a more effective and inspiring leader.

KEEP IN MIND THIS MONTH

Act on your own initiative instead of trying to figure out what others want and adapting your behavior to their needs.

KEY DATES

SUPER NOVA DAYS

★ **JULY 1–3**

roll up your sleeves

An enthusiastic Mercury-Jupiter quincunx on **July 1** can overload your mind with data or your schedule with activities. No matter how fascinating a conversation might be, ask yourself if it's really necessary: Today, simplicity is the key to productivity. Hardworking Mars entering ethical Virgo and your 7th House of Partnerships is another reason to stay on top of things. Showing up on time and performing at your peak potential build trust in relationships. A more playful mood prevails with an extravagant Venus-Jupiter opposition on **July 3** that promises pleasure and delight. The cost in cash, calories, or concentration may be high—but it's probably worth it.

★ **JULY 9–10**

back to earth

An opposition between the expressive Sun and benevolent Jupiter on **July 9** opens your heart and raises your hopes. However, you must follow up on big promises from friends or co-workers to keep them from fading away unfulfilled. A hard-core conjunction between Mars and stern Saturn on **July 10** imposes limits that separate fantasy from reality. Relationships can be tested by a lack of trust or by mounting stress. If you value the connection, stay calm, be practical, and focus on fixing the situation rather than adding more emotional fuel to the fire.

★ JULY 15

lost in space

Favorable aspects from the Sun and Mercury to energetic Mars make for some zippy thinking, but moving too quickly can lead you astray. Foggy Neptune's disorienting aspects to the Sun and Mercury may cloud your judgment with idealism that's not grounded in reality. Apply your imagination in spiritual or creative ways where strict adherence to the rules is not necessary.

★ **JULY 18–19**

relationship accounting

The rational Capricorn Full Moon on **July 18** can open your eyes to see where you truly stand with your friends. Make a point of acknowledging those who support you with some appreciative words. Notice those who take more than they give and start changing the equation to make it more balanced. Talkative Mercury has plenty to say with an opposition to wide-open Jupiter on **July 19**. Exaggeration is possible, and you could easily blow little details out of proportion. If you feel anxious, take a breath and reassess before letting emotions go too far.

★ **JULY 26**

bold steps

You can speak with confidence as Mercury enters brash Leo on **July 26**. A high-energy Mars-Jupiter trine provides integrity and enthusiasm, giving you the power to successfully sell your ideas. This physical planetary pair also encourages vigorous activity, making this a fantastic time to explore the great outdoors.

AUGUST

PARTNERSHIP POTENTIAL

A pair of eclipses and two New Moons make this an unusually transformative month. The Solar Eclipse in fixed Leo on **August 1** in your 6th House of Work and Service could produce a tiring battle of wills on the job. Yet if you let go of your expectations, you can discover a creative solution in which everyone comes out ahead. A Lunar Eclipse in unorthodox Aquarius on **August 16** sends your imagination off into fantasyland. Psychic Neptune's conjunction to the Full Moon floods your 12th House of Spirituality with images and feelings of worlds beyond this one. Don't act impulsively on these impressions or try to make sense of them now. Allow yourself time to absorb this nonlinear information before making any major changes. The New Moon in analytical Virgo on **August 30** brings relationship issues into focus with a crystalline clarity that signals exactly where you stand and helps you make a logical decision.

Three planets enter virtuous Virgo and your 7th House of Relationships this month, bringing new opportunities to connect with others. Sociable Venus starts the process on **August 6**, drawing appreciative individuals into your life. Thoughtful Mercury follows on **August 10**, opening the door to more reasonable dialogue that helps you work through complicated issues in a calm and rational manner. The life-giving Sun moves into Virgo on **August 22** to increase your confidence, gain the support of creative allies, and encourage you to express yourself more boldly within one-to-one relationships and in dealing with the general public. Verbal Mercury enters your 8th House of Intimacy on **August 28**, followed by creative Venus on **August 30**, taking personal and professional partnerships to a deeper and more powerful place.

KEEP IN MIND THIS MONTH

Thoughtless and unkind remarks tend to undermine trust, but constructive criticism can be a major asset for building stronger relationships.

KEY DATES

★ **AUGUST 1–2**

round and round

Drama at work triggered by the showy Leo Solar Eclipse in your 6th House of Employment on **August 1** can blow a small issue into a major event. Humor and generosity are the keys to turning a potential tragedy into an outright comedy. On **August 2**, communicative Mercury skids off a quincunx with Jupiter, the multiplier, which can drag discussions off track by mixing up facts with opinions. If a conversation starts going around in circles, stop it or change the subject to avoid wasting time or wearing yourself out.

★ **AUGUST 6**

no rules

Romantic Venus's entry into cautious Virgo and your 7th House of Partnerships normally indicates a careful step forward in relationships. But the situation is far from stable: Mental Mercury is firing up your nervous system in a quincunx to electric Uranus while Mars opposes it, instigating impulsiveness and possible outbursts of anger. Tense aspects to boundless Jupiter and imprecise Neptune lure emotional communications far from reality. Chaos and confusion diminish your confidence in others, yet this can be a powerfully creative time when there are no rigid expectations to follow.

SUPER NOVA DAYS

★ **AUGUST 13–16**

relationship dilemma

A hard, cold Venus-Saturn conjunction on **August 13** can put a chill on relationships, but don't give up on love. If you aren't receiving the appreciation you desire, state exactly what you want. Be prepared to invest in a partnership for the long term—or start thinking about a way to escape. Your imagination is wide open with a Sun-Neptune opposition on **August 15**, but a rigid Mercury-Saturn conjunction can confront you with an individual who only deals in facts. The gulf between you may feel vast, yet a generous trine between lovely Venus and jovial Jupiter on **August 16** can drive away despair by revealing an unlimited source of joy.

★ **AUGUST 21–23**

social surprise

A sweet Mercury-Venus conjunction on **August 21** draws you into pleasant conversations, while the Sun's entry into discerning Virgo on **August 22** may attract a powerful ally. Meanwhile, oppositions from Mercury and Venus to "wild and crazy" Uranus on **August 23** can evoke irrational behavior. Unusual individuals or your own unexpected impulses can be exciting but destabilizing. Stay open-minded and light on your feet, Pisces, to adjust to the sudden changes.

★ **AUGUST 28–29**

transforming love

Mercury's entry into diplomatic Libra on **August 28** opens the way to meaningful negotiations, yet an intense square between sensual Venus and disruptive Pluto on **August 29** stirs deep emotional waters. A sense of loss or betrayal might undermine trust; however, sharing these feelings without shame or blame can heal a significant relationship and restore your sense of self-worth.

SEPTEMBER

RIDER ON THE STORM

Just as long-range plans seem to be lining up logically, an unexpected event or change of heart can lead to a major course shift this month. Jupiter and Saturn align in an organizationally gifted trine on **September 8** for the second time this year, bringing a healthy balance of optimism and realism to your life. This stabilizing aspect occurs for the third time on **November 21** to complete a building process that started last year. Your newly earned security, however, is interupted by an explosive Full Moon in your sign on **September 15**. Full Moons always raise emotional tides, yet this one is especially volatile: Uranus, the planet of shock, rebellion, and breakthrough, is closely conjunct, releasing unexpected circumstances and unpredictable responses. You may be bored with routine, restless for change, and ready to turn your life upside down. It's also possible that you're comfortable where you are—but the world around you suddenly seems to start spinning in the opposite direction. Regardless of how fast things turn, your intuition can respond quickly enough to keep up.

Ordinary thinking just isn't good enough with cerebral Mercury slowing down as it heads toward its retrograde period, which starts on **September 24**. The Sun's entry into accommodating Libra and your 8th House of Intimacy on **September 22** brings you assistance from objective individuals who can offer you wise counsel. Seductive Venus plunges into the emotional depths of Scorpio on **September 23**, where she helps restore a sense of purpose to your life. The Libra New Moon on **September 29** in your 9th House of Higher Truth lifts your spirits and invites you on a philosophical quest.

KEEP IN MIND THIS MONTH

*If you keep a light hand on the wheel,
the road will tell you which way you need to turn to
avoid accidents and safely reach your destination.*

KEY DATES

★ **SEPTEMBER 3–8**

set the stage

The creative Sun's passage over strategic Saturn on **September 3** and trine with lucky Jupiter on **September 4** provide you with insights and allies to manifest your ambitions. Still, a sloppy Venus-Neptune sesquisquare on **September 5** puts hope before reason and can obscure your judgment. A highly energized square between aggressive Mars and Jupiter on **September 7**, however, propels you forward with great force. Tense aspects to your key planet Jupiter on **September 8** fire you up with strong opinions that can provoke clashes. This is also the day of the Jupiter-Saturn trine, as Jupiter turns direct—a pivotal point when the decisions you make can have lasting effects.

SUPER NOVA DAYS

★ **SEPTEMBER 12–15**

chaos and change

A jumpy Sun-Uranus opposition on **September 12** can surprise you as a reliable person fails to perform as expected, a shy friend turns bold, or even you take uncharacteristic risks in sharing your true feelings. **September 14** looks like a slippery Sunday with a Sun-Neptune quincunx better suited for escapism than practical pursuits. The powerful Pisces Full Moon on **September 15** is electrified by its conjunction to Uranus, while a tense square to the Sun and Moon from extreme Pluto makes this an even more transformational time. There's too much happening for you to comprehend at once; keep things simple rather than adding fuel to the raging fire. Small moves have major effects, so temper your responses to maintain some semblance of control.

★ SEPTEMBER 17
love heals

A sweet Venus-Neptune trine brings pleasure to soothe the rawness of your emotions. This can be an island of calm in the midst of the swirling waters of change. Indulge in a healthy escape—go shopping, or lose yourself in a feel-good movie—to take your mind off life's larger challenges. Moments of delight with an easygoing person remind you of the healing power of love.

★ SEPTEMBER 20–22

pros and cons

A compelling square between the Sun and Pluto on **September 20** brings buried issues to the surface. Power struggles and feelings of resentment aren't your idea of fun, but they can show you what's really important so you can clear out what you don't need and concentrate your efforts where they count. A creative trine between assertive Mars and idealistic Neptune on **September 21** demonstrates that self-interest and spirituality can be compatible. Sharing the day with supportive friends makes the differences between work and play disappear. The Sun enters fair-minded Libra on the Autumnal Equinox, **September 22**, showing you that it is possible to see both sides of a situation without losing your center.

OCTOBER

HUNGER TO LEARN

Your personal life heats up this month with Venus and Mars, the cosmic lovers, changing signs. Physical Mars turns more passionate on **October 4** when it enters Scorpio, a fellow water sign bound to warm up your emotions. Its passage through your 9th House of Faraway Places urges you to expand your horizons and, perhaps, express discontent with your current situation. Sensual Venus moves into freedom-loving Sagittarius and your 10th House of Public Status on **October 18**, which tends to put you in the spotlight. Your artistic abilities and people skills garner respect that increases your sense of self-worth, making you even more popular. The spontaneous Aries Full Moon on **October 14** in your 2nd House of Resources could send you on an impromptu shopping spree, but a spark of originality that generates new sources of income is a more useful expression of this energizing event.

Rational Mercury turns direct on **October 15** to get discussions moving forward with a new line of thinking. Negotiations in your personal or professional life open up with fresh perspectives that help overcome barriers to communication. The unyielding Sun enters Scorpio and your 9th House on **October 22**, adding conviction to your beliefs and passion to your presentations. You may appear to be less flexible when it comes to matters of principle if others pressure you. Fortunately, when you're allowed to explore on your own, an obsessive curiosity can motivate you to examine religion, philosophy, or politics through study and travel. The New Moon in penetrating Scorpio on **October 28** deepens your desire to understand your life and enrich it with meaning. Although a charismatic teacher may influence your thinking, put more trust in your own innate instincts to find the truth.

KEEP IN MIND THIS MONTH

Tune in carefully to what others are saying and you'll discover the best way to satisfy their needs while also fulfilling your own desires.

KEY DATES

SUPER NOVA DAYS

★ **OCTOBER 4–6**

stop and go

Mars's passionate push into intense Scorpio on **October 4** can lead directly to an obstacle when it makes a tense semisquare to restricting Saturn on **October 5**. If you aren't getting the support you need, be very clear about what you want instead of silently bearing the burden alone. Venus's semisquare with extreme Pluto can undermine trust and leave you scrambling for resources. Fortunately, the tide starts to turn as a positive sextile between Venus and Jupiter encourages you with a helping hand. Extravagant squares from the Sun and Mercury to Jupiter on **October 6** may find you susceptible to exaggeration, unrealistic promises, or an information overload. The Sun's conjunction with retrograde Mercury can tie you up with someone who's stuck on an old idea. If reason doesn't work, postpone further discussion instead of allowing frustration to increase.

★ OCTOBER 11

the curse of pollyanna

A fuzzy square between attractive Venus and nebulous Neptune turns up the volume on your fantasies. Acquaintances appear more alluring, and worthless objects glitter like gold. Seeing the best in everyone and everything is one of your greatest talents, but your judgment may be especially unreliable now. Avoid a tendency to sacrifice your needs to make others happy, no matter how much you care.

★ OCTOBER 14–15

limited resources

The fiery Aries Full Moon on **October 14** is superheated by a square to overdoing Jupiter and supported by Neptune and the Sun. If you volunteer in a group situation or offer to help a friend, set some realistic limits rather than making an open-ended commitment. Mercury's direct turn on **October 15** is a perfect time to stop and take a fresh look at a relationship before getting in over your head.

★ OCTOBER 21–22

quiet strength

You have the ability to ask for more from others as a savvy Sun-Pluto sextile on **October 21** clarifies your desires. Your strong convictions send a message that doesn't require shouting to make your point. The Sun's entry into fellow water sign Scorpio on **October 22** imbues your actions with a deeper sense of purpose.

★ OCTOBER 26–28

true believer

Direct Mercury square gregarious Jupiter on **October 26** can make you very chatty, or possibly indiscreet. Be careful talking about friends or colleagues—even an innocent remark may be perceived as gossip. Active Mars's friction-free sextile with outgoing Jupiter on **October 27** increases your enthusiasm, enabling you to be a strong motivator, skillful team leader, and effective spokesperson for your ideas. The New Moon in magnetic Scorpio on **October 28** charges your beliefs with heartfelt intensity, sending you on a quest to spread the word wide and far.

NOVEMBER

ENDINGS AND BEGINNINGS

There's a cosmic changing of the guard this month: Two long-term planetary patterns end, and a new one begins. Rigid Saturn opposes revolutionary Uranus on **November 4**, starting a series of aspects that will continue through **July 26, 2010**. This tense angle between the principles of order and chaos has a major impact on how you connect with others. The urge to break free from the constraints of judgment and guilt may upset or even dissolve a partnership. If you don't act impulsively, however, this can be a manageable step toward overcoming the limits you experience within a current relationship or your beliefs about creating a new one. Jupiter makes the last in a series of smart sextiles with Uranus on **November 13** and its final trine with Saturn on **November 21** to inspire an exciting vision for the future and to provide you with a strategic, organized plan to turn it into reality.

Two planets turning direct add waves of forward movement. Dreamy Neptune leads off on **November 1** to externalize your spiritual aspirations; then inventive Uranus releases lightning bolts of originality on **November 28**.

Additionally, five planets change signs this month, shifting the colors of your personal landscape. Perceptive Mercury's entry into Scorpio on **November 4** deepens your thinking to reveal underlying motives. Stylish Venus turns formal in Capricorn on **November 12**, requiring clarity about what you want from friends and within groups. Adventurous Mars shoots into Sagittarius and your 10th House of Career on **November 16**, encouraging risk taking in your professional life. When the Sun follows Mars's path on **November 21**, you can express your intentions openly and act more confidently in public. Powerful Pluto reenters ambitious Capricorn on **November 26**, where it will powerfully redefine and reshape your position in groups for years to come.

KEEP IN MIND THIS MONTH

No matter how irritated you are by an obstinate person, gentle persuasion will be more effective than an emotional eruption.

KEY DATES

★ **NOVEMBER 3–5**

relationship breakthrough

Relationships are rattled when affectionate Venus bounces off squares from Saturn to Uranus on **November 3**. Feelings of rejection incite strong emotions to break free of restrictive patterns in partnership and release some of the building tension of the Saturn-Uranus opposition due **November 4**. A misguided Mars-Neptune square can stir up misplaced anger or an attempt to escape reality. However, your exquisite sensitivity can provide the compassionate touch needed to diffuse a volatile situation. A gentle Venus-Neptune sextile on **November 5** reveals common ground to overcome the ache of separation.

SUPER NOVA DAYS

★ **NOVEMBER 10–13**

practical genius

Use your willpower and creativity wisely when the Sun harmonizes with Jupiter, Uranus, and Saturn on **November 10–11**, connecting unconventional concepts with logical thinking to turn brilliant ideas into reality. You could see your trust in someone shaken on **November 12** when Venus conjuncts Pluto; express your dissatisfaction if you can do so without going to extremes. Venus then enters responsible Capricorn, where relationships and self-worth improve with discipline and diligence. The Full Moon in sensual Taurus on **November 13** opens your eyes to delights in everyday life. A Sun-Neptune square, though, can lead to self-sacrifice, illusions about your capabilities, or promises that will be hard to fulfill.

★ NOVEMBER 16–17

strategic thinking

Mars motivates you to try harder professionally when it enters enthusiastic Sagittarius on **November 16**. This urge to advance is intelligently supported by sextiles from Mercury to successful Jupiter and pragmatic Saturn. Your sense of strategy is excellent, as is your ability to share your thoughts with authority without sounding aggressive. Ideas, however, may become less clear on **November 17** when

Mercury squares misty Neptune. Don't make assumptions; double-check your facts to ensure the accuracy of what you say or hear.

★ **NOVEMBER 21**

change for the better

The final Jupiter-Saturn trine occurs as the Sun enters long-distance Sagittarius to set your sights on a brighter future. Trust yourself: You now have the right balance of hope and realism to reinforce long-term constructive changes to your life.

★ **NOVEMBER 27–28**

information indigestion

The outspoken Sagittarius New Moon on **November 27** in your 10th House of Public Status marks a time to express your opinions more openly. However, holiday conversations can slide off point with destabilizing semi-squares between detailed Mercury and "big picture" Jupiter on **November 27** and the Sun and Jupiter on **November 28**. Taking in more data than you can digest or making outrageous statements can reduce your credibility.

DECEMBER

SERIOUS ABOUT GETTING AHEAD

A combative Sun-Mars conjunction on **December 5** in your 10th House of Career can stir up conflict on the job. Regardless, this may be an excellent time to launch a new project if you nail down the necessary details in advance. Vivacious Venus enters Aquarius and your 12th House of Privacy on **December 7**, which can pull you away from your usual social circle. You might appreciate more time alone or with spiritual groups, where you feel less judged and are free to be yourself. Mental Mercury enters constructive Capricorn on **December 12**, helping you turn inspiring ideas into concrete events, yet the chatty Gemini Full Moon may resist the Capricorn call for order. The natural mobility of the Sun in Sagittarius opposing the Moon in Gemini is heightened by a tense square with electric Uranus. An impulse to change your job, drop an obligation, and seek greener pastures is understandable. Meanwhile, responsible Saturn's square to the Full Moon reminds you that tossing aside one obstacle may present you with another one, so create a workable plan before making a sudden move.

The Sun enters traditional Capricorn and your social 11th House on **December 21**, marking the Winter Solstice and bringing your attention to group activities just in time for the holidays. A harsh square between the Sun and compulsive Pluto on **December 22**, however, can produce power struggles, but is more creatively expressed by eliminating superfluous activities that distract you from your heart's desire. Resentment of others may seem justified, but it's not an effective way to spend your resources. The New Moon in ambitious Capricorn on **December 27** is conjunct a potent Mars-Pluto conjunction that can bring you the support of powerful allies . . . if you just ask for their help.

KEEP IN MIND THIS MONTH

You can achieve great things if you focus on yourself and let your ambition fuel the fire in your belly.

KEY DATES

★ **DECEMBER 5–6**

tempestuous thoughts

A brilliant but erratic Mercury-Uranus square on **December 5** spawns unusual ideas and strange conversations that make the day's forceful Sun-Mars conjunction even hotter. Tempers can flare easily if misunderstandings bring unresolved grievances to the surface—so choose your words carefully. A strict square from Saturn to Mercury on **December 6** stops wild speculation and demands down-to-earth communication. A kind Mercury-Neptune sextile follows to soften hearts and allow for less rigid thinking.

SUPER NOVA DAYS

★ **DECEMBER 10–13**

boiling over

The brilliant yet explosive power of Uranus enters the foreground with harsh aspects to the Sun, amicable Venus, and excitable Mars on **December 10–12**. These high-frequency alignments of rebellion and restlessness are likely to upset your equilibrium. The positive potential for intuitive breakthroughs, new pleasures, and innovative problem solving requires a cool head to keep your nervous system from overheating. The Full Moon in versatile Gemini on **December 12** adds tension, especially if restrictive Saturn's square to the Moon is totally resistant to change. You are unlikely to be in a compromising mood, so unless you want a crisis to escalate, it's wise to back off. A sweet sextile between the Sun and Neptune on **December 13** adds tolerance and awareness to help you find mutual common ground.

★ DECEMBER 15–16
sigh of relief

A two-day two-step of planetary pressure and release occurs with a hard square between Mars and stern Saturn on **December 15** and a relaxed sextile between Mars and pliable Neptune on **December 16**. The action planet passes from a tight squeeze where there is no margin for error, especially at work, to an easygoing attitude that values peace and imagination more than productivity.

★ **DECEMBER 21–22**

stay in charge

Group responsibilities weigh heavily when the Sun enters your 11th House of Teamwork on **December 21**. Take command and control the process as much as you can rather than trying to make everyone happy. The Sun's square with unrelenting Pluto on **December 22** reveals that if you aren't totally on top of a situation, you may wind up buried by it. Concentrate on business now and you can play later.

★ **DECEMBER 27–28**

total commitment

Mars enters industrious Capricorn just before the New Moon in this earthy sign on **December 27**. These indicators of seriousness and hard work can serve your highest ideals in the company of an inspired Venus-Neptune conjunction. If you're going to exert maximum effort, make sure it's for something you truly value. Mars joins Pluto on **December 28**, which can also focus intense power in a narrow beam. If you dedicate yourself fully right now, you can make lasting changes.

APPENDIXES

★

2008 MONTH-AT-A-GLANCE
ASTROCALENDAR

★

FAMOUS PISCEANS

★

PISCES IN LOVE

TUESDAY 1

WEDNESDAY 2

THURSDAY 3

FRIDAY 4

SATURDAY 5

SUNDAY 6 ★ Apologize and move on if you stumble verbally through the 8th

MONDAY 7 ★

TUESDAY 8 ★

WEDNESDAY 9

THURSDAY 10

FRIDAY 11

SATURDAY 12 ★ Keep the faith and you'll find boundless hope

SUNDAYY 13

MONDAY 14

TUESDAY 15

WEDNESDAY 16 ★ Your compassionate heart heals wounded feelings

THURSDAY 17

FRIDAY 18

SATURDAY 19

SUNDAY 20 ★ **SUPER NOVA DAYS** Unexpected help arrives through the 22nd

MONDAY 21 ★

TUESDAY 22 ★

WEDNESDAY 23

THURSDAY 24

FRIDAY 25

SATURDAY 26

SUNDAY 27

MONDAY 28 ★ Don't escape into diversions through the 30th

TUESDAY 29 ★

WEDNESDAY 30 ★

THURSDAY 31

FRIDAY 1 ★ Mix business and pleasure successfully through the 2nd

SATURDAY 2 ★

SUNDAY 3

MONDAY 4

TUESDAY 5

WEDNESDAY 6 ★ You possess the power necessary to save yourself

THURSDAY 7

FRIDAY 8

SATURDAY 9

SUNDAY 10 ★ Avoid making promises while you're lost in wonderland

MONDAY 11

TUESDAY 12

WEDNESDAY 13

THURSDAY 14

FRIDAY 15

SATURDAY 16

SUNDAY 17 ★ **SUPER NOVA DAYS** Narrow your focus through the 20th

MONDAY 18 ★

TUESDAY 19 ★

WEDNESDAY 20 ★

THURSDAY 21

FRIDAY 22

SATURDAY 23

SUNDAY 24 ★ A reality check puts relationships to the test

MONDAY 25

TUESDAY 26

WEDNESDAY 27

THURSDAY 28

FRIDAY 29

SATURDAY 1

SUNDAY 2

MONDAY 3

TUESDAY 4

WEDNESDAY 5

THURSDAY 6 ★ **SUPER NOVA DAYS** Lightning may strike through the 9th

FRIDAY 7 ★

SATURDAY 8 ★

SUNDAY 9 ★

MONDAY 10

TUESDAY 11

WEDNESDAY 12 ★ Through the 15th, relationships may fluctuate when you gain clarity

THURSDAY 13 ★

FRIDAY 14 ★

SATURDAY 15 ★

SUNDAY 16

MONDAY 17

TUESDAY 18

WEDNESDAY 19

THURSDAY 20 ★ Let go rather than fight through the 21st

FRIDAY 21 ★

SATURDAY 22

SUNDAY 23

MONDAY 24

TUESDAY 25

WEDNESDAY 26 ★ Add chills and thrills to your social life through the 28th

THURSDAY 27 ★

FRIDAY 28 ★

SATURDAY 29

SUNDAY 30

MONDAY 31

TUESDAY 1

WEDNESDAY 2

THURSDAY 3

FRIDAY 4

SATURDAY 5 ★ Calculate the risks before leaping now

SUNDAY 6 ★

MONDAY 7 ★

TUESDAY 8

WEDNESDAY 9

THURSDAY 10 ★ Take what you hear with a grain of salt, even from friends

FRIDAY 11

SATURDAY 12

SUNDAY 13 ★ **SUPER NOVA DAYS** Hope floats, but don't go overboard now

MONDAY 14 ★

TUESDAY 15

WEDNESDAY 16

THURSDAY 17

FRIDAY 18

SATURDAY 19

SUNDAY 20

MONDAY 21

TUESDAY 22

WEDNESDAY 23 ★ You want more, more, more through the 24th

THURSDAY 24 ★

FRIDAY 25

SATURDAY 26

SUNDAY 27

MONDAY 28 ★ Postpone decisions until you have more information

TUESDAY 29 ★

WEDNESDAY 30

THURSDAY 1

FRIDAY 2 ★ Stick to the facts and back them up with proof through the 3rd

SATURDAY 3 ★

SUNDAY 4

MONDAY 5

TUESDAY 6

WEDNESDAY 7 ★ Stretch your mind, but avoid overstatement

THURSDAY 8

FRIDAY 9

SATURDAY 10

SUNDAY 11

MONDAY 12 ★ Be true to your heart now

TUESDAY 13 ★

WEDNESDAY 14 ★

THURSDAY 15

FRIDAY 16

SATURDAY 17

SUNDAY 18 ★ **SUPER NOVA DAYS** Find a brilliant way out through the 22nd

MONDAY 19 ★

TUESDAY 20 ★

WEDNESDAY 21 ★

THURSDAY 22 ★

FRIDAY 23

SATURDAY 24

SUNDAY 25

MONDAY 26

TUESDAY 27

WEDNESDAY 28

THURSDAY 29

FRIDAY 30

SATURDAY 31

SUNDAY 1

MONDAY 2

TUESDAY 3 ★ Communication from family or friends brings joy now

WEDNESDAY 4 ★

THURSDAY 5

FRIDAY 6

SATURDAY 7

SUNDAY 8

MONDAY 9

TUESDAY 10

WEDNESDAY 11

THURSDAY 12

FRIDAY 13 ★ Forget about an old issue instead of fighting through the 15th

SATURDAY 14 ★

SUNDAY 15 ★

MONDAY 16

TUESDAY 17

WEDNESDAY 18 ★ **SUPER NOVA DAYS**

Impetuous acts take you off track through the 26th

THURSDAY 19 ★

FRIDAY 20 ★

SATURDAY 21

SUNDAY 22

MONDAY 23

TUESDAY 24

WEDNESDAY 25 ★ Foolish illusions have consequences through the 26th

THURSDAY 26 ★

FRIDAY 27

SATURDAY 28

SUNDAY 29

MONDAY 30

TUESDAY 1 ★ **SUPER NOVA DAYS** Get to work through the 3rd

WEDNESDAY 2 ★

THURSDAY 3 ★

FRIDAY 4

SATURDAY 5

SUNDAY 6

MONDAY 7

TUESDAY 8

WEDNESDAY 9 ★ Be practical! Come back down to earth now

THURSDAY 10 ★

FRIDAY 11

SATURDAY 12

SUNDAY 13

MONDAY 14

TUESDAY 15 ★ You feel lost in space when idealism clouds judgment

WEDNESDAY 16

THURSDAY 17

FRIDAY 18 ★ Balance relationships through the 19th

SATURDAY 19 ★

SUNDAY 20

MONDAY 21

TUESDAY 22

WEDNESDAY 23

THURSDAY 24

FRIDAY 25

SATURDAY 26 ★ Take bold steps to sell your ideas

SUNDAY 27

MONDAY 28

TUESDAY 29

WEDNESDAY 30

THURSDAY 31

FRIDAY 1 ★ Conversations can go in circles through the 2nd

SATURDAY 2 ★

SUNDAY 3

MONDAY 4

TUESDAY 5

WEDNESDAY 6 ★ Be creative when there are no expectations to follow

THURSDAY 7

FRIDAY 8

SATURDAY 9

SUNDAY 10

MONDAY 11

TUESDAY 12

WEDNESDAY 13 **SUPER NOVA DAYS** Don't give up on love through the 16th

THURSDAY 14 ★

FRIDAY 15 ★

SATURDAY 16 ★

SUNDAY 17

MONDAY 18

TUESDAY 19

WEDNESDAY 20

THURSDAY 21 ★ Stay on your toes through the 23rd. Surprises are in store

FRIDAY 22 ★

SATURDAY 23 ★

SUNDAY 24

MONDAY 25

TUESDAY 26

WEDNESDAY 27

THURSDAY 28 ★ Sharing your feelings can heal a relationship through the 29th

FRIDAY 29 ★

SATURDAY 30

SUNDAY 31

MONDAY 1	
TUESDAY 2	
WEDNESDAY 3 ★	Decisions made through the 8th have a lasting effect
THURSDAY 4 ★	
FRIDAY 5 ★	
SATURDAY 6 ★	
SUNDAY 7 ★	
MONDAY 8 ★	
TUESDAY 9	
WEDNESDAY 10	
THURSDAY 11	
FRIDAY 12 ★	**SUPER NOVA DAYS** Chaos fuels change through the 15th
SATURDAY 13 ★	
SUNDAY 14 ★	
MONDAY 15 ★	
TUESDAY 16	
WEDNESDAY 17 ★	Indulge in a healthy escape
THURSDAY 18	
FRIDAY 19	
SATURDAY 20 ★	Supportive friends can help keep you centered through the 22nd
SUNDAY 21 ★	
MONDAY 22 ★	
TUESDAY 23	
WEDNESDAY 24	
THURSDAY 25	
FRIDAY 26	
SATURDAY 27	
SUNDAY 28	
MONDAY 29	
TUESDAY 30	

OCTOBER 2008

WEDNESDAY 1

THURSDAY 2

FRIDAY 3

SATURDAY 4 ★ **SUPER NOVA DAYS** Be clear about your needs through the 6th

SUNDAY 5 ★

MONDAY 6 ★

TUESDAY 7

WEDNESDAY 8

THURSDAY 9

FRIDAY 10

SATURDAY 11 ★ Avoid your tendency to sacrifice for the happiness of others

SUNDAY 12

MONDAY 13

TUESDAY 14 ★ Set realistic limits now

WEDNESDAY 15 ★

THURSDAY 16

FRIDAY 17

SATURDAY 18

SUNDAY 19

MONDAY 20

TUESDAY 21 ★ Your actions are fueled by quiet strength through the 22nd

WEDNESDAY 22 ★

THURSDAY 23

FRIDAY 24

SATURDAY 25

SUNDAY 26 ★ Heartfelt intensity charges your beliefs through the 28th

MONDAY 27 ★

TUESDAY 28 ★

WEDNESDAY 29

THURSDAY 30

FRIDAY 31

SATURDAY 1

SUNDAY 2

MONDAY 3 ★ Break free from restrictive patterns through the 5th

TUESDAY 4 ★

WEDNESDAY 5 ★

THURSDAY 6

FRIDAY 7

SATURDAY 8

SUNDAY 9

MONDAY 10 ★ **SUPER NOVA DAYS**
Apply discipline and diligence through the 13th

TUESDAY 11 ★

WEDNESDAY 12 ★

THURSDAY 13 ★

FRIDAY 14

SATURDAY 15

SUNDAY 16 ★ Your sense of strategy is heightened through the 17th

MONDAY 17 ★

TUESDAY 18

WEDNESDAY 19

THURSDAY 20

FRIDAY 21 ★ Hope helps you make long-term constructive change

SATURDAY 22

SUNDAY 23

MONDAY 24

TUESDAY 25

WEDNESDAY 26

THURSDAY 27 ★ Don't take in more data than you can digest through the 28th

FRIDAY 28 ★

SATURDAY 29

SUNDAY 30

MONDAY 1

TUESDAY 2

WEDNESDAY 3

THURSDAY 4

FRIDAY 5 ★ Choose words carefully when thoughts race through the 6th

SATURDAY 6 ★

SUNDAY 7

MONDAY 8

TUESDAY 9

WEDNESDAY 10 ★ **SUPER NOVA DAYS** Restlessness boils over through the 13th

THURSDAY 11 ★

FRIDAY 12 ★

SATURDAY 13 ★

SUNDAY 14

MONDAY 15 ★ Breathe a sigh of relief now

TUESDAY 16 ★

WEDNESDAY 17

THURSDAY 18

FRIDAY 19

SATURDAY 20

SUNDAY 21 ★ Stay on top of business through the 22nd

MONDAY 22 ★

TUESDAY 23

WEDNESDAY 24

THURSDAY 25

FRIDAY 26

SATURDAY 27 ★ Make a total commitment to lasting change through the 28th

SUNDAY 28 ★

MONDAY 29

TUESDAY 30

WEDNESDAY 31

FAMOUS PISCEANS

Seal	★	2/19/1963
Smokey Robinson	★	2/19/1940
Cindy Crawford	★	2/20/1966
Kurt Cobain	★	2/20/1967
Robert Altman	★	2/20/1925
Ansel Adams	★	2/20/1902
Nina Simone	★	2/21/1933
Erma Bombeck	★	2/21/1927
George Washington	★	2/22/1732
Drew Barrymore	★	2/22/1975
Luis Buñuel	★	2/22/1900
W. E. B. DuBois	★	2/23/1868
Dakota Fanning	★	2/23/1994
Steve Jobs	★	2/24/1955
George Harrison	★	2/25/1943
Johnny Cash	★	2/26/1932
Tony Randall	★	2/26/1920
Elizabeth Taylor	★	2/27/1932
Joanne Woodward	★	2/27/1930
John Steinbeck	★	2/27/1902
Chelsea Clinton	★	2/27/1980
Ron Howard	★	3/1/1954
Ralph Ellison	★	3/1/1914
Roger Daltrey	★	3/1/1944
Harry Belafonte	★	3/1/1927
Karen Carpenter	★	3/2/1950
Dr. Seuss	★	3/2/1904
Mikhail Gorbachev	★	3/2/1931
Jon Bon Jovi	★	3/2/1962
Jackie Joyner-Kersee	★	3/3/1962
Jean Harlow	★	3/3/1911
Alexander Graham Bell	★	3/3/1847
Antonio Vivaldi	★	3/4/1678
Niki Taylor	★	3/5/1975
Shaquille O'Neal	★	3/6/1972
Elizabeth Barrett Browning	★	3/6/1806

FAMOUS PISCEANS

Alan Greenspan	★	3/6/1926
Kathy Ireland	★	3/8/1963
Micky Dolenz	★	3/8/1945
Freddie Prinze, Jr.	★	3/8/1976
Bobby Fischer	★	3/9/1943
Juliette Binoche	★	3/9/1964
Bow Wow	★	3/9/1987
Chuck Norris	★	3/10/1940
Sharon Stone	★	3/10/1958
Rupert Murdoch	★	3/11/1931
Sam Donaldson	★	3/11/1934
Darryl Strawberry	★	3/12/1962
James Taylor	★	3/12/1948
Liza Minnelli	★	3/12/1946
Jack Kerouac	★	3/12/1922
Edward Albee	★	3/12/1928
Neil Sedaka	★	3/13/1939
L. Ron Hubbard	★	3/13/1911
Quincy Jones	★	3/14/1933
Michael Caine	★	3/14/1933
Albert Einstein	★	3/14/1879
Eva Longoria	★	3/15/1975
Mia Hamm	★	3/17/1972
Nat "King" Cole	★	3/17/1919
George Plimpton	★	3/17/1927
Vanessa Williams	★	3/18/1963
Queen Latifah	★	3/18/1970
Glenn Close	★	3/19/1947
Bruce Willis	★	3/19/1955
Fred "Mr." Rogers	★	3/20/1928
Spike Lee	★	3/20/1957

PISCES IN LOVE

PISCES–ARIES (MARCH 21–APRIL 19)

By nature, you're quite sensitive and aware of the subtle currents of energy surrounding you, and often have artistic and musical abilities. Rams are individualistic, with a tremendous amount of courage and stamina. They can be impatient and may tend toward angry outbursts. The two of you can be quite different. In some ways, when you hook up with a fiery Aries, it will be like oil and water. Yet you can lend a calm and sympathetic perspective to the Ram, softening his or her sometimes harsh and self-centered ways. And, the intense and focused drive of your mate can spur you into action in ways you've never imagined. Problems can arise when you feel pushed too hard by the unyielding will of your Aries mate, while he or she may get impatient with your unrealistic ways. If you have Mercury or Venus in Aries, or the Moon in any fire sign, you'll naturally understand and accept Aries's sometimes abrasive actions, thereby increasing chances for compatibility. It's vitally important that headstrong Aries doesn't bully you into following his or her agenda. Your Ram will have to accept your sensitive and tender nature.

PISCES–TAURUS (APRIL 20–MAY 20)

You go with the flow, enabling you to get along with people who are more headstrong than yourself. In relationships, you need to hold your own power so that others can't take advantage of your sweet nature. You don't have the same stubborn personality as the Taurus in your life, but always giving in to his or her needs may feed your sense of martyrdom. Bulls are mighty in their pursuit of accomplishment. They love to feel as though they possess everything around them. Actually, this all bodes well for you. You admire your Taurean's stability and ability to work in the real world, yet you also appreciate the underlying attraction of sensuality and beauty. You're able to move through the currents of their stubborn nature with uncanny grace. Your Taurus partner is a loving sign by nature. He or she is less threatened by you than by other signs and is able to soften in your presence and to surrender to your emotional needs. Your chance for compatibility is increased if your chart has Venus in Capricorn or the Moon in any earth sign. The two of you can create a loving, beautiful home. As romantic partners, you two can be very compatible, bringing sensual and emotional enjoyment to each other in a lasting relationship.

PISCES–GEMINI (MAY 21–JUNE 20)

You are quiet and love to indulge in the mystical, meditative aspects of life. You are highly intuitive and can feel the pulse of other people's thoughts and energies. Your communication can be subtle, sometimes through music, poetry, or dance, which enables you to cross the threshold of the material world into the sublime realms of spirituality, religion, and art. When you fall for a restless and verbally active Gemini, your cage feels rattled. Twins are mental by nature. They are the word wizards of the zodiac and possess great language skills. The two of you have much in common, yet you tend to work with the energy in very different ways. You both move about frequently and may actually have many jobs, homes, or relationships. You'll respect each other's need for stimulation, although your Gemini lover may seem too noisy at times. If Gemini can incorporate your quieter inner mystical needs with his or her clever communication style, you two can be quite entertained by each other. Your chances for long-term happiness are increased if you have the Moon or Mars in an air sign. In an intimate relationship, you two will be best off if you read, write, meditate, and share your visions with each other.

PISCES–CANCER (JUNE 21–JULY 22)

Your key planet is Neptune, the god of the seas. You live in a diffused ocean of feelings, and your love for animals, children, and nature has no bounds. In your Cancer mate you find a long-lost friend, for the Crab is also a water sign, connected with the Moon. The Moon symbolizes the changing tides of emotions and as such, your nurturing Cancer lover may exhibit changeable moods. Cancers need a warm and cozy home in which to thrive. Together, you're comfortable with your feelings and show tender care to one another, family, and friends. One area of concern is that you may both lack the ability to deal with real-world issues, preferring to retreat into your private haven. Your acute sensitivity to the Crab's moods can actually drive you to the depths of despair. But, with the Moon or Mars in a fire or air sign, you'll inspire your worrisome partner to move beyond his or her emotional restraints, which in turn frees you from depression. If you and your Crab decide to go for it, you'll create a lovely home together. This can be one of the best unions, as both of you are willing to share your innermost self with each another, providing a context from which you can engage the routines and tests of the real world.

PISCES–LEO (JULY 23–AUGUST 22)

Quiet, dreamy, and imaginative, you need reflective time to remain centered and balanced. Meanwhile, Leo is dramatic, outgoing, and is most comfortable in groups where recognition is available. It's not that your Leo lover always needs to be the center of attention, but he or she can become vulnerable if not acknowledged within a social context. The two of you are different and it will take some significant adjustments for both of you to find a firm foundation on which to stand together. You are sensitive to the vulnerable aspects of Leo's personality, and may be able to salve the big, tender heart of your proud Lion. But your lover may demand more from you than you can give, causing you to withdraw into fantasy realms. You'll probably be pulled into the limelight whether you want it or not. If you have Venus in Aries or the Moon in any fire sign, you'll be better equipped to handle all the social activity. Your Leo mate will need to learn to give you the quiet time that you require. When Leos are balanced and aware, they tone down the demands they place on others and place value on building their self-confidence from within. When this happens, you and your Leo mate can build a more lasting and meaningful union.

PISCES–VIRGO (AUGUST 23–SEPT. 22)

Virgo is opposite you on the zodiac wheel, and in many ways is a mirror image for you. Even though some of your traits are polar opposites, you seem to be mutually attracted to each other. You're dreamy and imaginative, and operate from a nonrational, emotional perspective. Virgo is detail-oriented, efficient, and rational. With so many differences, it would seem as if you two would never get along, but it is quite common to find this pair in a very successful relationship. Your life is enhanced by Virgo's organized ways if you let them help you to order your surroundings so you can materialize your dreams and visions. If the Moon or Mars in your birth chart is in an earth sign, you'll better appreciate your Virgo mate's sense of practicality, which can enhance your chances for compatibility. Meanwhile, you help to open your Virgo lover's heart and teach them how to experience compassion and empathy. You both care deeply about service to others. If the two of you can find a common ground from which to operate, you'll be able to assist each other in the process of creating a life of goodwill and service, while growing personally into realms that are opposite your normal way of living.

PISCES–LIBRA (SEPT. 23–OCT. 22)

Boundary issues are sometimes difficult for you Pisces folks. You can sacrifice much in order to help your partner in any way you can. Your intuitive guidance and empathy can help heal the emotional, spiritual, or physical wounds of your friends, family, and coworkers. When you hook up with a Libra, you may initially feel as if you've met someone who is as good at relationships as you are, but Libras are air signs, and as such can be emotionally detached. This doesn't feel right to you—you live your life swimming in a sea of feelings and when they're taken away, you feel like a fish out of water. If you have the Moon or Mars in an air sign it may be easier for you to accept the easy-going nonemotional style of your Libra lover. Your Libra partner will need to feel united with you as part of a team. If you do have areas of common interest, the two of you can be very good together because you both want to help those you love. Libras are conscientious, with refined tastes. You're also attuned to the beautiful and sublime, and want a mate who can appreciate life's finer things. Neither of you is overly materialistic, but you'll probably live in nice surroundings, leading each other into a life of greater awareness and joy.

PISCES–SCORPIO (OCT. 23-NOV. 21)

You are acutely aware of the suffering taking place on a global level, even if your own surroundings are safe and loving. As such, Pisceans are often involved in volunteer programs. In Scorpio, you find someone who can go to the very depths of the emotional well with you. Scorpios carry intense concern for the world and are often involved in work projects that delve into the hidden mysteries of life, for that is where they see potential for fixing the world's ills. Your Scorpio lover may be forthright and reliable when functioning from their highest potential, but when facing their own emotional fears, Scorpios can be stone cold and secretive, hiding their feelings deep within, where they can be controlled. Both of you are water signs and your styles of engaging the world are compatible. Your Scorpio lover is highly responsive to your universal concerns while you're understanding of his or her fiery passions. You may have difficulty with practical issues unless your Moon or Mars is in an earth sign. Your relationship is a romantic one and if you choose to share your life together, the odds are in your favor. You'll need to teach your lover how to forgive and forget, and in turn you'll learn how to live life to the fullest.

PISCES–SAGITTARIUS (NOV. 22–DEC. 21)

You are a true visionary with an active imagination that stimulates your desire to be of service to all beings on the planet, yet you may find it a challenge to implement your ideas. All that changes when you meet a goal-oriented Archer, who's happiest when pursuing a long-held dream. Sagittarians are able to work tangibly with their ideas and bring them to fruition. Like you, they're idealists who aren't afraid to commit to a greater cause. Although problems may arise because your styles are so different, you can assist each other a great deal. A Sagittarius partner can help you achieve your goals while you're able to fuel him or her with a wealth of imaginative material with which to work. Together you'll have a good sense of humor; you'll appreciate the undying optimism of your inspirational mate. Sagittarians can be self-righteous and you may get angry if you feel like you're not being taken seriously. If the Moon or Mars in your chart is in an earth sign, you may have more of a practical lean and this won't be a problem. If your Venus is in Aries, compatibility is increased. Regardless of other planets, this can be an excellent union if you each allow the other room enough to bring their true gifts to the relationship.

PISCES–CAPRICORN (DEC. 22–JAN. 19)

Pisces are highly sensitive and ethereal, and not always able to feel secure in the world around you. It can be of great benefit to you if you have a partner who can ground and support your efforts, giving you a stable base from which to live your life in imaginative ways. Capricorn can do that. Goats are practical and goal-oriented. They have a serious and hard-working nature. Your Capricorn lover is a grounded earth sign who is most content while pursuing tangible tasks. There could be issues—your Goat may not trust your intuition and may see you as a lost soul—but there is also an upside to this relationship. Capricorn is able to help you to be more effective in the outer world. If, however, you have the Moon or Mars in an earth sign, you may not be so dependent on your partner for help with practical affairs. You may even have some things of your own to teach them! You also show serious Capricorn the rich worlds of imagination and spirituality. You get to teach your mate about tenderness while he or she helps you bring your visions and dreams into reality. You're very compatible, but your feelings may be hurt if your lover is too demanding. Most likely, you'll find a path that make the best of both worlds.

PISCES–AQUARIUS (JAN. 20–FEB. 18)

When you become involved with an Aquarian, at first it seems like you two are so very different: your reality is emotional; his or hers is intellectually detached. You may be quite compatible in philosophy, but different in your style of execution. You are aware of global suffering and pain, and Aquarius wants to do something about it. You are both evolved and aligned with a higher understanding, and try to bring love and tenderness into your relationships, yet with a nonpersonal edge. You are both probably interested in programs that promote goodwill, and may even meet at a volunteer organization. Your emotional world coupled with your Aquarius lover's mental emphasis creates a need to balance the intuitive and intellectual sides of your nature. If Venus in your chart is in Aries—or better yet—in Aquarius, you'll adapt more easily to life with an emotionally cool Aquarius. If the Moon or Mars in your chart is in an air sign, chances for compatibility are improved even more. There can be a strong bond between you two that goes deeper than the eye can see with a harmonious resonance on a very high note. This can be a good match if you both strive for awareness and stay on a spiritual path.

PISCES–PISCES (FEB. 19–MARCH 20)

Sometimes, it's difficult for you to find other people who understand the breadth of your compassion and your vulnerable sensitivity. It's not always easy for you Fish to live in the material world because you are so naturally attuned to the invisible ripples in the seas of life. This is why some Pisceans may lean toward escapist addictions. But you can also choose to escape the mundane world by indulging in spiritual or creative pursuits. When you hook up with another Fish, you'll need to focus on building a stable foundation. At first, you may feel as though you are looking into the magical eyes of your soulmate. In time, however, you may find that staring into the eyes of your beloved can only last so long, for there are mouths to feed and bills to pay. Your biggest challenge will be to find ways to ground yourselves in the very world that you choose to escape from. If the Moon or Mars in your chart is in an earth sign it may be easier for you to deal with responsibilities. Even so, you'll need to create regular routines that enable you to manifest your dreams. Together, you share a love of the arts and sensual lovemaking. This is a beautiful match as long as you make the mechanical parts work in the real world.

ABOUT THE AUTHORS ♓

RICK LEVINE When I first encountered astrology as a psychology undergraduate in the late 1960s, I became fascinated with the varieties of human experience. Even now, I love the one-on-one work of seeing clients and looking at their lives through the cosmic lens. But I also love history and utilize astrology to better understand the longer-term cycles of cultural change. My recent DVD, *Quantum Astrology*, explores some of these transpersonal interests. As a scientist, I'm always looking for patterns in order to improve my ability to predict the outcome of any experiment; as an artist, I'm entranced by the mystery of what we do not and cannot know. As an astrologer, I am privileged to live in an enchanted world that links the rational and magical, physical and spiritual—and yes—even science and art.

JEFF JAWER I'm a Taurus with a Scorpio Moon and Aries rising who lives in the Pacific Northwest with Danick, my double-Pisces wife, our two very well-behaved teenage Leo daughters, and two black Gemini cats (who are not so well-behaved). I have been a professional astrologer since 1973. I encountered astrology as my first marriage was ending. I was searching and needed to understand myself better. Astrology filled the bill. More than thirty years later, it remains the creative passion of my life as I continue to counsel, write, study, and share ideas with clients and colleagues around the world.

ACKNOWLEDGMENTS

Thanks to Paul O'Brien, our agent, our friend, and the creative genius behind Tarot.com; Gail Goldberg, the editor who always makes us sound better; Charles Nurnberg and Michael Fragnito at Sterling Publishing, for their tireless support for the project; Barbara Berger, our supervising editor, who has shepherded this book with Taurean persistence and Aquarian invention; Laura Jorstad, for her refinement of the text; and Sterling project editor Mary Hern and designer Rachel Maloney for their invaluable help. We thank Bob Wietrak and Jules Herbert at Barnes & Noble, and all of the helping hands at Sterling. Thanks for the art and ideas from Jessica Abel and the rest of the Tarot.com team. Thanks as well to 3+Co. for the original design and to Tara Gimmer for the cover photo.